African American News
in the
Baltimore Sun
1870 - 1927

Compiled & Edited
by
Margaret D. Pagan

CLEARFIELD

Published for Clearfield Company by
Genealogical Publishing Company
Baltimore, Maryland
2021

ISBN 9780806359335

Foreword

You are about to embark on a journey through African American History culled from the pages of the *Baltimore Sun*. Founded in 1837, with a goal of objectively reporting news devoid of political influence, the *Sun* published articles of local, national and international events relating to and impacting people of color.

The author has selected articles for this publication which provide an expansive overview of experiences chronicling the African diaspora. For example, the reader will learn of the evolution of "Jim Crow," regarding housing and interstate travel. Also included are summaries covering sports, lynching, entertainment, and political, educational, economic and religious activities. The accomplishments of well-known activists such as Frederick Douglass, and lesser-known ones such as Henry Highland Garnet, both Maryland born, are detailed.

This is an excellent source for genealogists as it presents names of marriage license applicants and obituaries, including names of officiating clergy and names of organizations to which the deceased belonged. Sadly, included also are the names of victims of torture and violence, along with details of their final hours. It is an excellent tool for educators, offering opportunities for students, at various levels, to sharpen research skills, interpret information and understand historical context. Finally, as an historian I found this work informative and entertaining.

Enjoy and learn from the experience Margaret D. Pagan has provided. I am hopeful that this is the beginning of a series of newspaper collections related to people of African descent.

Donna T. Hollie, Professor of History (retired) Sojourner-Douglass College, Baltimore, Maryland.

Introduction

This chronology does not attempt to cover every word written in the *Sunpapers* about African Americans. Rather it seeks to capture their spirit and the determination to pursue their own interests and live with equality and dignity during a critical time in history. Almost all articles summarized in the chronology contain more information than is given here.

When the guns of the Civil War fell silent, another battle began. Congress passed the 13th, 14th, and 15th amendments to the Constitution of the United States ushering in the Reconstruction Era. These amendments abolished slavery; provided for citizenship and equal protection under the law; and gave African American men the right to vote. In States such as South Carolina, with a large African American population, several men were even elected to political office.

The Ku Klux Klan, and other organizations and individuals, opposed Reconstruction and fought to enshrine their notion of white supremacy. They replaced "Slave Codes" with "Black Codes" designed to keep Blacks subservient. They terrorized freed slaves by assaulting, raping, and murdering them; shooting and burning their homes; and driving them off their land.

Many freed slaves left cruel Southern conditions and fled to northern states, Louisiana, Mississippi, and Indiana Territory. Thousands migrated to Africa and settled in the nation of Liberia. Those who stayed in the South fought the battle for justice and equality in what, for generations, had been their home. They fought wherever they were through feigned submission, subversion, open rebellion, and escape, all the while working and supporting their families.

The Africans brought to America as slaves may not, in many cases, have been the unlearned people they were thought to be. Missionaries had been working in African countries since the

1600's and had taught ideas in the Bible about freedom, justice, and equality. Other Africans were taught the Bible while enslaved, though plantation-owners carefully controlled what they learned. At the twenty-fourth anniversary of the Conference of the Missionary Society, it was reported that thirty to forty missionaries were engaged in the Carolinas, Georgia, Mississippi, and Louisiana, and that the colored population belonging to the fellowship and communion of the Church of God in these States numbered about 40,000.[1]

Maryland was unique among the States by having a higher population of free Negroes in 1835 than any other State.[2] Though it was not diligent in providing schools, free men and women were not forbidden from learning to read. This combination led to churches such as Sater's Baptist, being founded as early as 1742 in Howard County.[3] First Baptist Church in Baltimore sought admission to the Maryland Union Baptist Association in 1841.[4] And St. James laid its cornerstone in 1824. Early churches often had schools.[5] Once students had been taught, some taught others in their homes.

Readers will be horrified by the lengths that the Klan, other organizations, and individuals went through to destroy the Negro race rather than live beside them in freedom. Some historians state that more than 50,000 former slaves were killed by whites resisting the idea of racial equality.[6] But readers will be uplifted and filled with admiration for the way freed men and women, imbued with ideas of justice and equality, continued their fight for self-sufficiency day-by-day for the families they had raised, for the soil they had tilled, the crops they had harvested, the skills they

---

[1] *Baltimore Sun* Mar 13, 1844
[2] *Baltimore Sun* Feb 07, 1985
[3] *Baltimore Sun* Feb 10, 1987
[4] *Baltimore Sun* Oct 22, 1841
[5] *Baltimore Sun* Jul 06, 1887
[6] https:/www.smithsonianmag.com/history/terrorized-african-americans-champion-civil-war-hero-robert-smalls-1809770031/

had learned, and the nation they had helped build. They believed they had enough to fight for. They stood on the foundation of the Black Church and carried its banner. This chronology includes not only the names of the fearless and esteemed leaders of the battle, but also names men and women who excelled in their areas of endeavor, and of ordinary working people. It will, hopefully, serve as a primary resource for genealogists, researchers, scholars and historians for years to come and excite interest in heroes previously unknown. Capitalization of most words, and the terms Colored or Negro, are used as they were in the newspaper at the time.

Though published in Baltimore, the *Sun* covered many events along the Eastern Seaboard from Florida to New England and a few other States. It ends in 1927 because of copyright requirements but we are thankful for the news within its pages. We laud the victories we have won but we also know that the battle goes on.

Acknowledgements

This book began when I approached Dr. Donna T. Hollie with a stack of clippings about Black history mostly from the *Sunpapers* that I had accumulated over the years. My interest in Black history began during the 1960's when both Dr. Hollie and I were students at Morgan State College. While I became a genealogist and writer, she became a historian. So when I showed her my clippings, she said, "I know someone who will publish those." That led to a discussion of possibilities with the publisher and we agreed on a chronology extending from 1870 to 1970. I failed to realize that this amounted to 36,500 pages that I had to review. When it became overwhelming, Barbara Cooper and Phyllis Jenkins stepped in to pray for me and encourage me. Keionna Stewart helped to organize my pages. When the publisher informed me that the book would be printed from what I submitted, Tonda and Ariana Stanton helped me with the computer-related aspects of preparing the manuscript for printing. I was later informed that I would be charged for each *Sunpaper* article in which I used more than 10 percent of the content. Only articles up to 1927 were in the public domain. This reduced the book to so few pages that I wanted more, and Carolyn Brown helped. When the end was finally reached, an index had to be added which could not have been done without help from my daughter Carla Pagan. So, together, we created this book.

Date of Publication	Event
Jan 03, 1870	A republican president, Abraham Lincoln, issued the Emancipation Proclamation effective January 1, 1863 freeing 3.5 million people held as slaves in States rebelling against the federal government. On this date, it was celebrated in Richmond, Virginia.
Jan 04, 1870	Jane Loane, residing in the seventh ward in Washington, D.C. died at the advanced age of 100 years. She was originally from Northumberland County, Virginia.
Jan 11, 1870	Following Emancipation, many freed slaves wanted to leave the South. Unnamed agents helped them leave to fill the need for laborers in Indiana Territory. Some lamented the loss of "industrial capital" when thousands of former slaves left Virginia.
Jan 19, 1870	The American Colonization Society held its fifty-third anniversary meeting in New York. Hon. John H.B. Latrobe of Baltimore and others delivered reports. The Society's ship *Golconda* sailed for Liberia last November with one hundred and sixty emigrants. They were in the prime of life and mostly farmers. Twenty-six could read, and fifteen could read and write. Thirty-five were Baptist and eight Methodist. The Society had given passage to and settled 2,394 persons in Liberia during the previous four years. Applications were coming in from North Carolina and Louisiana for a Spring voyage. The stated goal of the Society was to construct a Christian African empire.
Feb 01, 1870	Rev. Hiram R. Revels served in Congress as the Senator from Mississippi from 1870 to 1871, filling a vacant seat. He was the first man of color to serve in that body. It is said that visitors in the galleries burst into applause as he entered the chambers to take his oath-of-office, knowing that they were witnessing history.[7]
Feb 01, 1870	Five colored men were taken out of jail and killed in Huntington, Carroll County Tennessee. One was named Mac Brown, another Allen Robinson.
Feb 12, 1870	It was announced at a meeting of republicans at the Broadway Institute in Baltimore that Congress ratified the 15th amendment to the Constitution giving colored men the right to vote. Among the speakers were Dr. H. J. Brown, A. Ward Handy, Isaac Meyers, and Colonel William C. Saunders. The new voters expected that jobs as watchmen, inspectors, and postal workers would now become open to them.

[7] Freedmen were allowed to vote by the Mississippi State Legislature prior to ratification of the 15th amendment.

Feb 12, 1870	After observing the exceeding destitution and suffering of colored children without homes or protectors, several women presented a petition to the Maryland Legislature that led to the opening of a Shelter for Colored Orphans and Friendless Colored Children. Contributions were solicited and a liberal collection taken up. A housing address was made by Rev. J. B. Hawthorn of the Franklin Square Baptist Church.
Mar 02, 1870	A Negro was arrested in Stevenson, Alabama but taken afterward by the Ku Klux Klan and carried off. He was supposed to have been killed. Soldiers arrived from Huntsville to investigate the affair.
Mar 08, 1870	The Postoffice Department appointed Isaac Meyers as a special agent at large at $1,200 per annum and $3 per diem.
Mar 08, 1870	Senator Hiram R. Revels of Mississippi spoke at Bethel Church, on Saratoga Street between Holiday and Gay. About thirty white leaders were present by invitation. He spoke of the war and of the ratification of the 15th amendment and said that it was a practical demonstration of the great Lawgiver that we are all of one blood and ought to unite in the political progress of humanity. He further said that education was the great lever by which to raise and enable the African race.
Mar 24, 1870	Squatters defied authorities and caused troubles near Hampton, Virginia.
Apr 01, 1870	A colored man of foreign birth who had lived in the U.S. for 40 years was denied citizenship because of his race. U.S. Senator Charles Sumner, a strong supporter of Civil Rights, said he had introduced a bill to end discrimination in naturalization laws and that it was before the judiciary committee.
Apr 05, 1870	The election of five commissioners required for Towsontown to be incorporated as a town became the first occasion in Maryland for colored men to vote. Though the polls did not open until noon, they began gathering at the polling site in early morning. William Taylor was the first of thirty-seven jubilant colored men who'd registered, and the first to vote was Elijah Quigley.
Apr 28, 1870	Despite considerable opposition from students, President Ulysses S. Grant appointed James Taylor as postmaster at the University of Virginia near Charlottesville.
May 19, 1870	The colored population of the city and State planned a grand demonstration in honor of the ratification of the 15th amendment to the Constitution, which secured men's right of suffrage throughout the country. The Philadelphia Excelsior Cornet Band composed of upward of twenty members and led by Capt. Edward Johnson arrived by train accompanied by some thirty delegates who joined the large party.

May 28, 1870	A charter required each inhabitant of Chestertown, Maryland to be the owner of real estate in the town before he could vote in the election for county commissioners. Colored men were each deeded an inch of worthless ground, voted, and The Party of Lincoln won by a large majority.
Jul 08, 1870	J. W. Smith of Hartford, Connecticut was cursed, insulted, and abused while a cadet at West Point. Classmates harassed him when he slept, ate, and drilled. His complaints to the commandant did not resolve the issues and he eventually resigned.
Aug 03, 1870	In a letter to the Honorable R.M. Pearson, Chief Justice of the Supreme Court of North Carolina, Governor Holden said in part, "I have official and reliable information that in the counties named above during the last twelve months not less than one hundred persons 'in the peace of God and the State' have been taken from their homes and scourged, mainly if not entirely on account of their political opinions; that eight murders have been committed, including that of a State Senator, on the same account; and that another State Senator has been compelled, from fear of his life, to make his escape to a distant State. I have reason to believe that the governments of the said counties have been mainly if not entirely in the hands of men who belonged to the Ku Klux Klan whose members have perpetrated these atrocities referred to and that the county governments ….actually shielded them from arrest and punishment….this organization is known as "The White Brotherhood"…."[8]
Aug 18, 1870	Two hundred fifty people were helped by unnamed agents to leave Richmond, Virginia and emigrate to Boston and other parts of New England to fill the demand for cooks, maids, and dining room servants.
Aug 30, 1870	When the train he was riding reached Montgomery, Alabama, Sella Martin, a Federal officer representing the Post Office Department refused to move to the car assigned to colored passengers. The conductor called three men to lift him from his seat and take him there. When Martin later complained to railroad authorities, they expressed regret at the occurrence but excused themselves on the grounds that the orders of the directors were imperative. Martin then took his case to the United States District Attorney in Mobile who pronounced it one of the rarest cases of obstructing a United States officer that he had ever known and expressed a determination to enter a suit for $10,000 in damages.

---

[8] The State Senator killed by the Klan was John W. Stephens. He served as an agent of the Freedmen's Bureau and was hated by whites. See https://www.ncpedia.org/biography/stephens-john-walter

Aug 31, 1870	The Colored Democratic Association of which Jonathan Waters was president met at Zion Church, corner of Montgomery and Hanover streets.
Sep 01, 1870	Rev. D. P Seaton purchased tickets for seats in first class for himself and his wife at the Baltimore depot on the Western Maryland Railroad and was denied seating except in the colored car. They debarked intending to bring forward a claim for $10,000 damages.
Oct 10, 1870	A democratic mass meeting, under the auspices of the Colored Democratic Association of Baltimore was held in Annapolis. The meeting was largely attended by both white and colored, all advocating the election of Judge William M. Merrick as a Representative in Congress from Maryland. He won and was elected to Congress in 1872.
Nov 01, 1870	The *Golconda* sailed from Baltimore stopping at Hampton Roads to take on board 250 emigrants from North Carolina to join their friends in Brewerville City and Arthington, Liberia.
Nov 28, 1870	The Oblate Sisters of Providence, a Roman Catholic order of nuns founded in 1828 by Mother Mary Lange and Rev. James Joubert for the education of girls of African descent, held elaborate ceremonies attended by colored and white in connection with the laying of a cornerstone at their new location on Chase Street. They previously occupied a house on Richmond Street.
Dec 13, 1870	Joseph H. Rainey became the first of his race to be elected to the U.S. House of Representatives. A republican, he was sworn in to fill the vacancy when the former Congressman from South Carolina resigned. Rainey had previously become a member of the South Carolina State Convention and had served in the State Senate.
Dec 15, 1870	Rev. Jackson signified his acceptance of the call from the Madison Street Presbyterian Church.
Dec 26, 1870	Republicans in Georgia received a circular containing threats to everyone who intends to vote "illegally" by the command of the Grand Cyclops. "X Q Z Wizard of Chickamauga." At the top of the circular was the picture of a train with the word "blood" on a baggage car and "K.K.K." on a station house.
Jan 04, 1871	The Bureau of Refugees, Freedmen and Abandoned Lands, better known as the Freedmen's Bureau, created in 1865 to help freed slaves and poor whites in the South in the aftermath of the Civil War, reported that 1,500 freedmen were receiving food and shelter in Washington, D.C., that 1,087 bounties had been paid to colored troops, and that more than 2,000 schools and normal schools had been opened. Also, $25,000 had been

	transferred to Wilberforce University in Ohio, and $12,000 to Lincoln University in Pennsylvania by act of Congress.
Mar 16, 1871	In Virginia City, Nevada, 100 armed, masked members of the Ku Klux Klan took William Willis out of jail and hanged him to a beam until he confessed to attempting to burn Piper's Opera House and other crimes.
Mar 16, 1871	During the first session of the 42nd Congress, Representative Butler of Massachusetts read from a dispatch that the Ku Klux Klan of Mississippi had murdered four men. Representative Eldridge of Wisconsin said they killed more than that in New Hampshire.
Apr 22, 1871	The text of the Ku Klux Act which Congress passed on April 20th to impose heavy penalties against terrorist organizations and to use military force to suppress the Ku Klux Klan is reported here. The Klan used intimidation and violence to prevent freed slaves from exercising the rights granted by the 13th, 14th, and 15th amendments to the Constitution.
Apr 25, 1871	President Grant established a Commission, including Frederick Douglass, to investigate conditions related to annexing Santo Domingo to the U.S. Douglass gave a report of his trip to a large, racially-mixed audience at Bethel Methodist Church on Saratoga Street.
May 05, 1871	President Grant issued a proclamation stressing that officers of the law should be zealous in enforcing the Ku Klux Act throughout the nation due to the persistent violation of the rights of citizens.
Jul 21, 1871	J. C. Norris (white) testified before the sub-Committee investigating acts of the Ku Klux Klan that he had been elected sheriff of Warren County, Georgia in 1868 and served one year. He was compelled to leave the county by an organized band of the Ku Klux Klan. On one occasion, he was met and waylaid by five men, shot, and badly wounded. He also testified that a Dr. Darden had been put in jail while awaiting trial. A group of disguised men burned down the jail door to get him, took him out, and killed him. Witnesses fled the county and no one was punished for killing the doctor. Mr. Norris also gave accounts of other outrages including the murder of State Senator Atkins. The people, he said, are in terror and fear for their lives. Large numbers of colored men have gone to Mississippi, Louisiana, and other States where they deem they will be more secure.
Aug 26, 1871	According to the U.S. census of 1870, white residents numbered 605,497 in Maryland, and colored numbered 175,391.
Nov 11, 1871	An action was brought by John W. Fields against the Baltimore City Passenger Railway for $2,500 in damages for being put off one of their cars in which the sign: "Colored Persons Admitted Into This Car" did not appear. The jury ruled in favor of Fields though for a lesser amount.

Jun 27, 1872	Congress abolished the Bureau of Refugees, Freedmen and Abandoned Lands, better known as the Freedmen's Bureau, effective June 30th. The Bureau had provided food, housing, and medical aid; had established schools; and offered legal assistance to Negroes. The Freedmen's Hospital in Washington, D.C., however, was to be continued.
Jul 18, 1872	The Colored Republican Convention convened at Douglass Institute on Lexington Street to discuss whether to support Horace Greely or Ulysses Grant for President.
Aug 16, 1872	President Grant ordered pardons for six convicts of the Ku Klux Klan in Albany [Georgia] Penitentiary and was expected to pardon 18 more. It was unknown when and where they were convicted.
Sep 24, 1872	Appointed by Congressman Robert B. Elliott of the third district of South Carolina, John R. Conyers became the first Negro cadet at the Naval Academy in Annapolis. He was the subject of violent hazing, some from a cadet from Maryland who was dismissed from the Academy. Conyers later resigned.
Dec 20, 1872	The Sumner School, one of three schools for colored children in Washington, D.C., was so-named to honor white Massachusetts abolitionist and U.S. Senator Charles Sumner.
Sep 08, 1873	The Anne Arundel County republican convention met and elected R. P. Hunt as secretary. Thomas Young of Annapolis addressed the attendees and said that, if the votes were counted fairly, the republicans would have an overwhelming majority in the county notwithstanding the officials of the State against them. Both men were colored.
Jan 07, 1874	A Negro named Mr. Elliott of South Carolina, blessed with an unusually fine voice and a mind well-trained in excellent schools in Great Britain, spoke in the House of Representatives on behalf of the Civil Rights Bill of 1866.
Mar 05, 1874	Blanche K. Bruce, a republican and former slave, was sworn in as a member of the U.S. Senate from the state of Mississippi during an extra session. He was the first of his race to be elected and to serve a full term, which ended on March 5, 1881. The galleries were packed and hundreds of people were unable to get in.
Mar 05, 1874	The Senate resolved that P. B. S. Pinchback be admitted as a Senator from the State of Louisiana for the term of six years, beginning on the 4th of March, 1873. (He had won the election earlier but was denied his seat.)
Mar 14, 1874	The funeral of Senator Charles Sumner began with a procession from his residence to the Capitol. A guard of mounted police flanked the carriages and the hearse. Recognizing the fact that Senator Sumner's public life had been one of entire devotion to the colored race, and that his greatest

	efforts were put forth in their behalf, more than 300 colored people were assigned to positions in the procession nearest the hearse that bore his remains.
Apr 07, 1874	A drama in five acts entitled "The Family of Martyrs" was performed at St. Francis Xavier Church. Among the performers were A. Briscoe, J. Dorsey, and Ch. Madden. An orchestra played musical selections during the evening.
Apr 07, 1874	William A. Jackson died suddenly at his home at No. 10 Welch Alley. Coroner Mackall, being satisfied that death resulted from natural causes, did not hold an inquest. Jackson left a wife but no children.
Jun 16, 1874	Under the auspices of the Maryland Union Republican Association, a large meeting was held at Bethel African American Episcopal (A.M.E.) Church on Saratoga street in honor of the colored members of Congress: Joseph H. Rainy, Alonzo J. Ransier, and R. H. Cain of South Carolina; John R. Lynch of Mississippi; and P. B. S. Pinchback of Louisiana. Each Congressman spoke. When the meeting was adjourned, the majority proceeded to their homes while the Congressmen, with the band at the head of the procession, followed by members of the Association, marched from the church to Douglass Institute where a banquet was held. The supper hall was decorated with evergreens, flags, and portraits of Abraham Lincoln and Toussaint Louverture.
Jul 03, 1874	The Freedmen's Bank, established as part of the Freedmen's Bureau, went into liquidation despite efforts by Frederick Douglass and others to save it. Many former slaves were at risk of losing their savings.
Aug 26, 1874	At camp-meeting at Irving Park, Rev. William Thomas led the 8 o'clock prayer meeting, Rev. P.G. Walker preached at 10 o'clock, and Holy Communion was administered. Bishop Wayman held the audience spellbound at 3 o'clock, and many persons went forward. Rev. P.G. Walker was scheduled to hold a children's prayer meeting in the Dallas Street meeting tent the following day.
Nov 28, 1874	Romulus Moore, of Georgia, called for a convention of colored men to assemble in Atlanta to discuss moving to a Western state. He said he had heard of a Negro town in Texas with 1,600 inhabitants, its own government and taxes. He said the streets were paved, people lived in homes, and rode buggies, and carriages, and that all this had been described to him by a member of the Chattanooga Convention[9].
Feb 08, 1875	The Right Rev. H. Vaughn, Bishop of Salford, England, superior general of the mission to colored people of the United States, came to Baltimore

---

[9] According to the *Sun*, Oct 14, 1874 The Republican Convention had been held in Chattanooga, Tennessee.

	and preached at St. Francis Xavier Church, corner of Saratoga and Calvert Streets. He had toured the Southern States and gave his conclusions of the condition of the colored people there, dividing them into three classes. First were the utterly degraded, who in Mississippi and Louisiana were Voodoo worshipers, and seemed to be imbued with the powers of Satan; this class was few in number. Second, those who have no religion at all, numbering many thousands, and those who belonged to some sects that desired to do right, and serve God as well as they could. Third, the Catholics, many of whom had fallen away because of the want of priests to instruct them and be their pastoral guides. He found them often rising to great heights of sanctity and being great examples of the faith.
Feb 08, 1875	The State Board of Education reported that colored schools in the counties lack a suitable supply of school houses and competent teachers. The normal school for the education of colored teachers had two hundred and forty-six pupils during the year but the demand for such teachers was so great that it had been found difficult to keep students long enough in the school to become thoroughly qualified as teachers.
Mar 01, 1875	Congress passed a Civil Rights bill. The new law required that all persons within the jurisdiction of the U.S. shall be entitled to the full and equal enjoyment of the accommodations, advantages, facilities, and privileges of inns, public conveyances on land or water, theaters, and other places of public amusement; subject only to the conditions and limitations established by law, and applicable alike to citizens of every race and color, regardless of any previous condition of servitude. The second section provided that any person denied access to these facilities on account of race would be entitled to monetary restitution under a federal court of law.
Jul 08, 1875	Frederick Douglass along with Prof. John M. Langston, acting President of Howard University, delivered a 4th of July address at Hillsdale near Washington city.
Jul 26, 1875	The cornerstone of Allen Chapel on Stockton street, named after the first bishop of the A.M.E Church was laid. The congregation, now numbering over three hundred and fast-growing, was founded in 1859 by Rev. John M. Brown. The building as expected to cost $5,000.
Jul 26, 1875	The cornerstone of a small chapel called Henry's West Street M.P. Chapel on West street near Hanover street was laid. Singing was conducted by a choir led by T.A. Henry, a professor and composer of music There was a large congregation of white and colored people present. A liberal collection was taken to pay for the building.

	The Odd-Fellows met at St. Charles Hall on Saratoga Street near Gay to make arrangements for a parade and reception. Nearly all of the lodges of Baltimore were represented. Wm. Sprigg of the Humane Lodge, No. 1411 was elected chief marshal, and an association of butchers was to join the parade.
Aug 05, 1875	Shattered by grief and rage, hundreds of men and women crowded into a meeting at the Douglass Institute at the request of top community leaders. Lemuel G. Griffin called the meeting to order and John W. Locks was made chairman, while George Myers was chosen as secretary. I. O. B. Williams stated the details of the meeting. A few friends had gathered at the home of when they were alarmed by a furious knocking at the front door. When opened, a policeman entered and demanded to see the proprietor of the house, Daniel Brown, who explained the reason for the friendly gathering. The officer found Mr. Brown's reply impudent and struck his head so hard that he fell. His wife caught him and, seeing the policeman draw his revolver, begged him not to shoot. But the officer shot Brown in the head, killing him. The group called for judicial action and just punishment for the policeman who killed Daniel Brown.
Nov 16, 1875	The Freedmen's Savings Bank in Washington City was chartered by Congress in 1865 to encourage habits of frugality among persons previously held in slavery and their descendants. An amendment of the original charter was later procured however which enabled trustees to engage in "wildcat" activities that wasted the bank's money and led to its failure.
Nov 25, 1875	A trial was held in the case of police officer Patrick McDonald who shot and killed Daniel Brown in Brown's own home. When the jury first went out, it stood eight for a verdict of murder and four for manslaughter. The verdict was later changed to manslaughter, and the Criminal Court sentenced Patrick McDonald to the penitentiary for five years, which was less than the ten years required by law according to the Act of 1864.
May 20, 1876	The chairman of the select committee to investigate causes of the failure of the Freedmen's Savings Bank and Trust Company has submitted to the House of Representatives a report indicating that the bank was from the beginning a scheme of selfishness under the guise of philanthropy. The report gives a complete history of a certain swindle by which the bank lost $63,000 and recommends that the partners named in the report be punished to the fullest extent of the law.
Jul 18, 1876	Police officer Patrick McDonald was released from the penitentiary after five months by the Appeals Court on the grounds that his original

	sentence of five years was incorrect. He was required by law to serve not more than ten years or pay a fine of $500 with two years in jail, or both.
Aug 26, 1876	A mass meeting of colored republicans chaired by John H. Butler was held at the Douglass Institute. N.C.M. Groom, secretary, read the call for the meeting which was to consider what protection ought to be given to colored voters at the approaching election. It was stated that, for several years, the U.S. Marshall for the district of Maryland had failed in his duties, especially in October and November 1875. Colored voters had been deprived of the right to vote by armed and organized bands of men who intimidated and terrorized voters until they were driven from the polls. A change in marshals was deemed to be an absolute necessity.
Sep 9, 1876	A colored Hayes and Wheeler Club to support the candidacy of Rutherford B. Hayes and his running mate, William Wheeler, in the presidential election was formed in the seventh ward at Centennial Hall on Spring street. N.C.M Groom was elected president.
Oct 20, 1876	The colored Hayes and Wheeler Club of the ninth ward met at 38 Saratoga Street. John H. Coster served as president.
May 28, 1877	Mrs. Harriet Beecher Stowe said that no one person was described in "Uncle Tom's Cabin" as in biography. "The life of the Rev. J. Henson furnished many of these but not all. He was not Uncle Tom: neither was any other one person that I know of. Consequently, every person who has been trading at the British court or elsewhere on the assumption that he was the whole and individual Uncle Tom may be set down as fraud.
Jun 14, 1877	Henry O. Flipper, the fourth colored cadet to enter West Point, graduated. He said the professors had treated him justly, but that the other cadets did not want to speak to him. He received his commission as an officer but was told that the law required colored troops to have a white officer. His desire, he stated, was to be with colored troops.
Oct 03, 1877	Prof. John M. Langston departed to begin service as the U.S. Minister and General Consul to Hayti [Haiti].
Dec 10, 1877	Though P.B.S. Pinchback won the election for U.S. Senator from the state of Louisiana in 1873, he was denied his seat because of a dispute. After much discussion between involved parties, he retired from the contest.
Dec 10, 1877	Men traveling on the brig *Romance* met up with a schooner from St. Jago, Cuba near St. Domingo, which was headed for New York. Several men aboard the schooner were dead and others aboard suffered from yellow fever. Daniel Lovetts, Chas. Ford, Jacob Williams and James Fiske, all of Baltimore, helped get the schooner to New York and were promised $15 each when it arrived.

Dec 22, 1877	Citizen Charles Taylor applied for admission to practice as an attorney at law. The Court of Appeals unanimously decided that only white male citizens above the age of twenty-one years could be admitted to practice law in the State of Maryland. His application was refused.
Apr 22, 1878	About 250 people boarded the *Azor* in Charleston, South Carolina and began their voyage to Liberia. The Liberian Exodus Association coordinated the trip for those who wanted to leave the U.S. and return to Africa. Ironically, the ship, a clipper, was originally built for the slave trade. A correspondent from the *Charleston News and Courier* was one of only four white men aboard, and chronicled the adventures during the trip and after their arrival in the interior of Liberia.
Apr 10, 1879	Frederick Douglass spoke at City Hall in Frederick, Maryland before a racially mixed audience. In the course of his remarks, he referred to the exodus of his people from the South claiming that it was due to the effort of whites to force them back into a condition of slavery. In his advice to colored people, he said that there was no royal road to success. Honesty and integrity are the true means of excellency, and labor should be honored.
Aug 04, 1879	Methodist churches in Annapolis and Anne Arundel County held a camp meeting at Annapolis Neck.
Aug 04, 1879	Colored men have been employed on the streets of Annapolis since the republican administration went into power.
Sep 23, 1879	At the celebration of Emancipation Day in Cumberland, Maryland, the address was given by Frederick Douglass, the U.S. Marshall for the District of Columbia.
Sep 24, 1879	The Baltimore City School Board elected Sophia Brooks as an assistant teacher in female colored school No. 4.
Sep 24, 1879	Lillie Crier of No. 8 Peach Alley in Baltimore died. Born in Dorchester County, Maryland, she had reached age 108.
Sep 25, 1879	Colored republicans had demanded representation on the legislative ticket for an upcoming election. Though this was denied, John Briscoe was appointed a member of the campaign committee.
Sep 26, 1879	A crowd of 50,000 men, women and children gathered to celebrate the fiftieth anniversary of public schools in Baltimore City. There were in all 124 schools: 1 city college, 2 female high schools, 42 male and female grammar schools, 60 primary schools, 5 English-German schools, and 14 colored schools.
Feb 4, 1880	U.S. Senator Blanche K. Bruce and U.S. Marshall Frederick Douglass spoke before a racially mixed audience at the Presbyterian Colored

	Church on Madison Street about the "Progress and Future of the Colored Race in America."
Feb 23, 1880	By order of the presbytery, the Dolphin Street Presbyterian Church and the Constitutional Presbyterian Church combined to form the new Lafayette Square Presbyterian Church at Carrollton Avenue near Lanvale Street.
Apr 07, 1880	Three men broke into the room of Cadet Johnson C. Whitaker at West Point while he slept, and bound him hand and foot. One of the masked intruders said, "Let's mark him like they do hogs down south." They then cut the lower part of his left ear off and slit the lobe of his right ear. Despite the fact that Whitaker was found bloodied with his hand and feet bound, the final report concluded that his wounds were self-inflicted.[10]
Apr 08, 1880	Rev. C.B. Berry, rector of the Protestant Episcopal Church of St. Mary the Virgin inaugurated a meeting at the Samaritan Temple, North Calvert Street, to elicit support for an orphanage for colored boys. The orphanage had already been started at No. 20 Bolton Street and held six boys, but needed to be enlarged. John W. Locks presided at the meeting and addresses were made by Rev. J. H. Reddick, I.O.B. Williams, and Dr. Whitfield Winsey. A collection was taken and a committee appointed to continue raising money.
Sep 22, 1880	Samuel Diggs, age 26 of No. 11 Clarkson Alley, fell from a loaded guano cart which he was driving on Leadenhall street, and the wheel passing over his left leg broke it.
Sep 22, 1880	A committee had been appointed in April to confer with the board of public school commissioners in Baltimore about employing colored teachers in colored schools. The committee reported that they were satisfied with assurances given them by the board that their wishes would be complied with. Committee members were Rev. J. H. Reddick, Dr. H. J. Brown, J.W. Locks, J. H. A. Johnson, W.M. Hargrave, J. W. Beckett, and P. T. Gross.
Sep 22, 1880	The Baltimore City School Board reported that $9,271 had been paid toward expenses for white schools and $487 for colored.
Dec 18, 1880	Seven-year-old Samuel Johnson of 101 Jasper Street took a small seven-shooter pistol from his father's coat and accidently shot his sister Cora, aged 4. The ball glanced off his index finger and struck her in the forehead above the eyes, imbedding itself in the skull. Dr. F.P. Keller extracted the ball and the girl was doing well.

---

[10] American Heritage, Volume 22, Issue 55, August 1971.

Dec 20, 1880	A double funeral was held for John Meads and John Chew who were killed instantly as they walked home from work along the tracks of the Baltimore and Potomac railroad between Fulton and Lafayette stations. Services conducted by Rev. J. H. Reddick and attended by both races were held at Ames Chapel on Division Street.
Dec 20, 1880	Among the deaths reported by the city health office was that of Mrs. Amelia Bowers, age 88. The principal causes of death were consumption, pneumonia, scarlet fever, diphtheria, and croup.
Jan 31, 1881	The new building of the First Baptist Church at Caroline and Orleans Streets which seats approximately 1,200 was opened for services. Pastor J.C. Allen presided and sermons were preached by Rev. A. Brown of Leadenhall Street Baptist Church, Harvey Johnson of Union Baptist Church, and Rev. J.H. Reddick of Centennial Methodist Episcopal Church. The congregation had previously worshipped in a small building at Young and Thompson Streets.
Feb 21, 1881	The Baltimore County Colored Teachers Association met at the Howard Normal School building. James H. Scott was president and William H. Butler secretary.
Mar 07, 1881	All-day services were held at Orchard Street M. E. Church to raise funds to rebuild the church. In the morning Rev. James Thomas, pastor, preached; in the afternoon Rev. J. A.W. Brown of the Delaware Conference; and at night Rev. E. J. Adams of the Presbyterian Church, formerly a missionary to Africa.
Apr 26, 1881	A committee representing the colored soldiers and sailors of Maryland called on President Garfield. Consisting of John B. Briscoe, Isaac H. Baker, Samuel Young, E. M. Tilton, and Robert Burgess, the committee presented a resolution in reference to the claim of colored republicans to a proportionate share of federal patronage. They noted injustice and neglect at the hands of the republican party.
May 17, 1881	Bishops Payne and Wayman with twelve other preachers went to Cambridge to dedicate a new church and to attend the Maryland conference of the African Methodist Episcopal Church. Four deacons and two elders were ordained. Other appointments were made for the Baltimore, Hagerstown and Potomac districts. The next conference will be held at Ebenezer A.M.E. Church in Baltimore.
May 21, 1881	Rev. J. H. Reddick served as spokesman for William H. Bishop, Sr., Jacob A. Seaton, Dr. Whitfield Winsey, Dr. Henry J. Brown, Robert A. Stanley, John W. Locks, and George Lewis when they approached Postmaster Adreon about appointing more colored employees. Reddick stated that there were 1,720 federal appointments in

	Maryland of which 25 were held by colored men. The postmaster said he would look further into the matter. A second delegation headed by J.W. Reddy asked for better representation of colored voters of the third district in the post office.
May 21, 1881	The steamship *Koeln* arrived with 1,352 immigrants from Europe.
Jan 27, 1882	The *New York Times* estimated that 10,000 former slaves had emigrated from the State of South Carolina.
Jan 28, 1882	John Morris, aged 29 years, was hanged in Shelby, North Carolina for the murder of James Rourk. Four thousand persons witnessed the execution including about six hundred women. He confessed his crime and offered the following prayer. "Oh Lord, in Thy presence, I, a creature of moment present myself. I humbly beseech Thee to help me in this hour of death; help me to be strong and bear the agony of this hour--have mercy, purify and sanctify my heart; help and sustain me in this terrible trial. I ask a blessing on all men. Into Thy hands I commend my spirit." The trap was sprung and the fall of about five feet caused death by strangulation with blood flowing freely from the mouth, nose and ears.
Jan 28, 1882	The schooner *Cornelia Sparks* carrying a cargo of iron from Richmond to Baltimore capsized and sank near Norfolk. The bodies of Dick Reddick and Jim Johnson, who drowned at the mouth of the Nansemond river, were recovered. A third colored man survived.
Mar 09, 1882	Bishop William Pinkney confirmed a class of forty two candidates at the Chapel of St. Mary the Virgin Episcopalian Church.
Mar 09, 1882	The trustees of Madison Street Presbyterian Church on Madison Street between Park Avenue and Cathedral Street have contracted with Messrs. C.Y. Davidson & Co. to place new and handsome gas fixtures in their church. A new front of fine pressed brick has been put in the church edifice, giving the appearance of a new structure.
Mar 11, 1882	The late Rev. Henry Highland Garnet, said to be a fully African, was born in Maryland in 1817. His family escaped to Pennsylvania and he was able to get an education at the Oneida Institute in New York. He entered the Presbyterian ministry and became a noted member of the National Anti-Slavery Society. President Garfield later appointed him Minister to Liberia. He died in Monrovia and was buried with military honors.
Jun 28, 1882	Clergymen met at Douglass Institute to form an organization to promote the interests of colored people. Officers elected were as follows: President Bishop A.W. Wayman; vice presidents, Rev. J.H.A.

	Johnson and Harvey Johnson; secretaries, Revs. Palestine Henry and George W. Brodie; treasurer Rev. Robert Hawkins.
Aug 07, 1882	Thousands of worshippers packed trains leaving Calvert and Camden Stations for meetings at the following camps: Water's Grove in Baltimore County, Wesley Grove near Dorsey Station, Jackson Grove in Anne Arundel, Summit Grove in New Freedom, Pennsylvania, Irving Park at Annapolis Junction, and Chew's Woods near Towsontown.
Sep 14, 1882	Bishop A. W. Wayman presided at the Minister's Conference while Rev. Jacob Nicholson of St. John A.M.E. conducted opening exercises. Revs. Thomas Wells, Daniel Draper, and George W. Brodie of Baltimore were in attendance as well as delegates from Prince George's, Baltimore, Caroline, and Somerset counties. Rev. Jacob Strager from Salem, Massachusetts and others were also present.
Jan 25, 1883	Jerome Levi, who was injured on the Northern Central Railway, died at City Hospital of lockjaw.
Jan 25, 1883	The U.S. Supreme Court has under consideration the constitutionality of State laws prohibiting interracial marriage.
Jan 29, 1883	Ella Allison was severely burned on the right side while making a fire at her home, No. 70 Centre Market space.
Jan 29, 1883	Rev. A.C. Dixon preached at the ordination service for Rev. F.R. Williams at Perkins Square Baptist Church on Clinton Avenue and George Street. The church has about 200 members.
Jan 29, 1883	Charles Foote was sentenced to 60 days in jail and 7 lashes at the whipping post in Baltimore for wife-beating.
Feb 26, 1883	Sculptor Edmonia Lewis contributed her last known work, *Adoration of the Magi*, to the Episcopalian church, Chapel of St. Mary the Virgin, after having met the white missionary priest-in-charge, Rev. Calbraith B. Perry, at the Philadelphia Centennial Exposition.
Mar 15, 1883	Rev. J. Hudson Reddick, former pastor of Centennial M.E. Church at Caroline and Bank streets researched the church's history. He learned that the oldest Methodist church in Baltimore was the Strawberry Alley Methodist Episcopal Church on Fells Point. When the congregation outgrew the space, it gave the church over to colored congregants where it bore the name Dallas Street M. E. Church. On May 6, 1877 the Dallas Street congregation laid the cornerstone for a new church, Centennial. Frederick Douglass had attended the Dallas Street Church and was, along with other dignitaries, present for this event. The congregation moved to Centennial when the building was finished.

Oct 17, 1883	The U.S. Supreme Court ruled that the Civil Rights Act of 1875 was unconstitutional. The purpose of the Act was to assert the right of all persons to equal accommodations and privileges in hotels, in railroad cars, theaters and other places of public entertainment. In a consolidated case, known as the Civil Rights Cases, the court found that the 14th amendment to the Constitution granted Congress the right to regulate the behavior of States, not individuals.
Nov 30, 1883	Frederick Douglass lectured at the Centennial M.E. Church against the decision of the Supreme Court to rule the Civil Rights Act of 1875 unconstitutional. He said that the court chose to follow the letter of the law and not the spirit of the Constitution.
Nov 30, 1883	Samuel Snowden attempted to jump off a Baltimore and Potomac Railroad train at Glendale station but fell underneath a car. The wheels passed over his right foot crushing it terribly.
Apr 21, 1884	Rev. William H. Cole of the Maryland Bible Society was introduced to attendees at the Annual Conference of the A.M.E. Church and delivered an address on the work done by the Society in the past year. Revs. Herbert and W.H. Waters were, on motion, made life members of the Maryland Bible Society. It was noted that the law of the conference precluded acceptance of those who were slaves to the use of tobacco. Other business including a report on Sunday schools in the A.M.E. Church followed.
May 14, 1884	Bishop W. F. Dickson presided at the A.M.E. General Conference. In addition to the usual business of the Conference, Mrs. Frances Ellen Watkins Harper and Mrs. James Carey Thomas of the Women's Christian Temperance Union of Baltimore were presented, and gave addresses in advocacy of prohibitory laws. Also, a number of speeches on the death of Wendell Phillips, noted abolitionist, were made, eulogizing his services to freedom.
Jun 27, 1884	A delighted audience filled the Samaritan Temple to witness the closing exercises of the Baltimore Normal School for the Education of Colored Teachers. Among those present were two judges and a host of clergymen.
Jul 18, 1884	Officials from Baltimore conducted an inspection of the new House of Reformation for Colored Boys in Cheltenham, Prince George's County. The group included Rev. James Monroe Gilmer from the M.E. Church and Rev. James W. Danburry from Sharp Street Church. The facility measured 800 acres, contained 300 peach trees, and an apple orchard. It housed 224 inmates.

Oct 14, 1884	A *Sun* newsman reported on various colored secret societies that exist for the purpose of friendship and comradery, but whose principle object was to aid the sick and bury the dead. Two of the largest were the Galilean Fishermen headed by Thomas I. Hall and the Good Samaritans headed by Jacob A. Seaton. They both had meeting halls and together boasted about 8,000 members in Maryland.
Nov 28, 1884	George Briscoe was lynched by a party of masked men at New Bridge in Anne Arundel County following a series of robberies. He was described as being bright mulatto, 40 years old, and was married.
Nov 29, 1884	Articles collected by Rev. A. B. Wilson, Maryland commissioner on colored exhibits, were on display at his office, No. 30 North Calvert Street. They will be packed and shipped to New Orleans for exhibit at the World's Fair. Miss M. Howard of Baltimore contributed handsome decorative hand paintings, including work on a china cup and saucer. Miss Carrie L.L. Cook sent two worked pictures, one of a basket of fruit and another titled "The Incarnation of the Saviour." Other items from throughout the State included a fully equipped model of a steamboat, a locomotive, and crop specimens. Well-known citizens, Rev. C.W. Fitzhugh and Attorney Causeman H. Gaines, were very enthusiastic about the articles.
Dec 01, 1884	Carroll County reported that there were 128 public schools in the county, four of them for colored children.
Dec 06, 1884	The Methodist Episcopal (M.E.) Church was established at the Baltimore Christmas Conference in 1784, making Baltimore the birthplace of Methodism in this country. A planned centennial celebration expected about 500 delegates. Apart from the delegates who attended in an official capacity, more than 10,000 others were expected to be in the city.
Dec 15, 1884	Methodist Episcopal Sunday schools held a city-wide celebration of the Christmas Conference of 1784. Twenty-one different churches participated involving twenty-five thousand children. Among the churches were Centennial, Sharp Street, St. John, Trinity A.M.E., Metropolitan, Bethel, Ebenezer, John Wesley, St. Paul's, and St. James. Also Waters, Waugh, Allen, and Ames Chapels. Mission Sunday schools listed were Asbury, Metropolitan, Ames Chapel, St. Paul's, and St. James. The speakers at Centennial were Revs. J. A. Reed and B. T. Tanner; at Trinity, Revs. E. M. Hamilton and J. T. Jenner; and, at Metropolitan, Revs. J. C. Price and J. H. Nutter. Other churches had speakers and programs as well.

Dec 25, 1884	Under the direction of ex-Senator Blanche K. Bruce, the department for colored exhibits at the World's Fair held in New Orleans promised to be a great success. The idea of the display was not to separate the colored from the white people but to show the world what Negroes had made of their freedom. To afford every incentive for the fullest and most thorough exhibition, the board of management assigned the sum of $50,000.
Jan 05, 1885	The distinguished evangelist Dwight L. Moody (white) preached in the afternoon at the First Colored Baptist Church in Richmond, Virginia to a very large congregation.
Mar 02, 1885	William E. Matthews, a Washington lawyer, commended the *Sun* for its position on admitting colored men to practice law in the State courts of Maryland. He went on to compliment Maryland on being the only State that manumitted its slaves of its own free will [on November 1, 1864] months before the 13th amendment was passed.
Mar 21, 1885	Mr. John H.B. Latrobe addressed the Maryland Historical Society on the subject of Maryland in Liberia. He possessed deeds of land by the princes and headmen of Liberia given to the American Colonization Society. The oldest deed was dated April 12, 1821 and had been prepared at Jumbo Town in Grand Bassa. The King of Grand Bassa received tobacco, pipes, rum, cotton cloth, knives, spoons, beef, and other presents. At its January 19th meeting the Society reported that 15,736 emigrants from the United States had been set down there including 3,738 following the Civil War.
Mar 25, 1885	Charles Taylor's application for permission to practice law in Maryland was denied in 1877 because of his race. However, it bought attention to the application filed by Charles S. Wilson which had been pending for some time. The Supreme Bench decided in favor of admitting Wilson based on the 14th amendment to the Constitution. However, Wilson went away without availing himself of that right.
Jul 03, 1885	The Oblate Sisters of Providence held their 55th annual commencement for graduates of St. Francis Academy. There were 60 pupils in attendance representing 14 States and one from Cuba. Georgia Mordecai of Fernandina, Florida and Sarah Butler of Annapolis delivered addresses. Sister Theresa was the Mother Superior. An orphan asylum with 44 children was maintained in connection with the Academy.
Aug 07, 1885	Nearly 200 colored and white shipwrights, caulkers, and scrapers met at Von der Horst's Hall to form a protective union of all mechanics

	engaged in the construction of a ship. One colored caulker, George H. Hiner, spoke out and was applauded.
Sep 07, 1885	The health department recorded the death of Mrs. Lucinda Simmons, age 85.
Oct 10, 1885	Everett J. Waring of the District of Columbia who had been encouraged by Rev. Harvey Johnson, founder of Union Baptist Church, to come to Maryland and apply to practice law, did so, and became the first Negro admitted to practice law in Maryland courts. He was admitted to the bar of the Supreme Bench.
Oct 12, 1885	Alexander Haley went to sea at age 14. He was taught navigation by Capt. Richard Bennett and distinguished himself early on when captain and crew were taken ill while on a voyage from the East Indies. Haley brought the ship safely home. He commanded the schooner *George R. Macgill* for many years. Later, in the employ of the Maryland Colonization Society, he sailed the *Mary Caroline Stevens* and the *Golconda* to Liberia. Described as a man of ability and good qualities, he died at age 86.
Oct 12, 1885	In the obituary of Captain Alexander Haley, we are told that he left a wife and two daughters. All were educators. His wife conducted a school for forty years in the rear of their home on Dallas street. It was under her tuition that many representative men in the city received their education.
Jan 12, 1886	The Supreme Court rendered a judgement for $7,667 in favor of John M. Langston in his the government suit to recover the difference between his salary as minister to Hayti [Haiti] as fixed by law and the amount paid him under appropriations from Congress.
Mar 01, 1886	Joseph S. Davis, an attorney of the Supreme Court of the District of Columbia, became the second of his race admitted to practice law in Baltimore.
Apr 28, 1886	The Josephite Order of Catholic Priests were raising funds to build an orphan asylum for colored boys.
May 21, 1886	The *Charleston News and Courier* reported that Negroes in Charleston have $124,938 on deposit in five savings banks, the largest sum belonging to one person being $6,747 and the smallest $1.
Jun 08, 1886	Baltimore County recorded a real estate transfer from George Kephart to the Trustees of Reisterstown M. E. Church, part of a tract called Walnut Grove, for $94.
Feb 02, 1887	The Baltimore City School Board resolved in October 1882 to extend the Colored High School beyond two years. The superintendent was

	then instructed to prepare a curriculum for that school upon the same basis that prevails in white high schools.
Feb 23, 1887	Military parades marching from the Fifth Regiment Armory were enthusiastically greeted by crowds along the way. Followed by the white marchers were the colored military companies. First were the Monumental City Guards celebrating the fifth anniversary of their organization, numbering 61 members, who were organized in 1881 and mustered into service by the State in in 1882. The company occupied an armory on Mulberry street near Howard. The Monumental City Guards had 45 men in line, though their captain, Wm. R. Spencer was detained at home sick. The Monumental City Guards were joined by companies parading under the command of Captain George W. Matthews, the Lincoln Drum Corps, and the Baltimore Rifles. Next were 80 men of the Grant Memorial Guards under Captain James Flint. Finally marched the Baltimore City Guards under the leadership of Captain William Reed. All of the companies wore impressive uniforms and were said to have made a favorable impression.
Apr 08, 1887	The Order of Galilean Fishermen gave their first annual family reception and reunion at Raine's Hall. Rev. G. W. Watkins, pastor of Trinity A.M.E. Church, delivered an address of welcome, and was responded to by Thomas I. Hall, the right worthy national grand supreme ruler of the group. The Silver Star Cornet Band under the leadership of Capt. Brooks rendered music during the evening. Over 500 persons enjoyed the repast. Attendees are listed.
Apr 11, 1887	The roof of the old Dallas Street M. E. Church caught fire from a flying spark but was put out at slight loss.
Apr 16, 1887	Daniel Gittings was found dead in bed in his boarding house at 15 W. York street. Having recently returned from a trip down the bay, he had complained of feeling ill.
Apr 19, 1887	Rev. W.H. Weaver, pastor of Madison Street Presbyterian Church, sought to build a school and shelter in connection with his church and had raised $4,300 of the $5,500 needed for the shelter. He expects to receive the full amount and that the school will be put into operation in September next.
Apr 19, 1887	King Post Drum and Fife Corps, No. 33, Grand Army of the Republic (G.A.R.), entertained at Douglas Institute. By invitation, Lincoln Post a Drum Corps, No. 7, Guy Post Drum Corps, No. 6, G.A.R. the Brickmakers' Association, the Rosebud Assembly, the Middle Assembly, the Empire Club and Mt. Airy Social were also present in

	uniform. Music was rendered by the Empire Band. Promenading was led by George Williams, J. Wilson, and J. Sewell. The attendance was large.
May 11, 1887	The semi-annual meeting of the Maryland Literary Union convened at Metropolitan M.E. Church on Orchard street. W.T. Greenwood was president and Joseph Norris, secretary. Literary associations represented were: Asbury Lyceum, Centenary Biblical Institute Literary, John Wesley Lyceum, Magnolia Literary, Monumental, Roxana Literary, Sharp Street Lyceum, Waters Chapel Lyceum, Zion A.M.E. Literary, Thursday Evening Social, Ebenezer A.M.E. Lyceum, and Metropolitan M.E. Literary. The names of delegates were listed.
May 25, 1887	The Maryland Educational Union adopted a report submitted by Rev. W.M. Alexander and Attorney Joseph S. Davis citing the inadequacy of schools for colored children. The few schools available were overcrowded, in poor condition, and inaccessible to many children. The report noted that appropriations had recently been granted for a high school and a grammar school. It further stated that existing institutions for training teachers were insufficient and that teachers who were qualified had not received appointments. The report was prepared in response to misleading information issued by the school board,
Jun 08, 1887	For the first time in the history of Lincoln University, the son of a graduate received the title of A.B. and will follow the calling of his father, that of a minister. The father was Rev. Charles Hedges of Grace Presbyterian Church in Baltimore, and the son Charles S. Hedges. Also at the graduation, Charles W. Johnson of Baltimore gave the valedictory oration.
Jun 13, 1887	Col. John H. Alexander was the second to graduate from the United States Military Academy at West Point, New York.
Jun 24, 1887	With encouraging remarks, Mayor James Hodges presented diplomas to the graduates of Baltimore Normal School for the education of colored teachers.
Jul 06, 1887	Citing the lack of sufficient public schools, the members of Patterson Avenue Baptist Church were commended for opening its facility for a day school in 1885. It has served 350 children who pay 10 cents per week to attend, which constitutes the teacher's salary. The Rev. W.M. Alexander superintends the school. Henrietta Hucless, a graduate of Wayland Seminary in Washington, DC, serves as principal and Ida Johnson of Baltimore city high school and grammar school, the assistant.

Jul 07, 1887	The John Wesley M.E. Sunday school sponsored an excursion to Cambridge. More than 2,000 men, women, and children boarded the steamer *Emma Giles* and the steamer *Chester*. They were accompanied by the Silver Star Cornet Band lead by Prof. W. Scott.
Jul 18, 1887	A camp meeting of the Methodist Protestant churches in Baltimore began near Middle River Station on the Philadelphia, Wilmington, and Baltimore Railroad. The attendance numbered several thousand. The managers of the camp were Rev. W.H. Lee, pastor; Rev. A. Coupling, president; Rev. James Wells, secretary; and Rev. J.E. Hackett, superintendent.
Jul 18, 1887	Funeral services for Mrs. Eliza Jane Gillis, wife of Rev. Levi Gillis, pastor of Vincent Alley African Union Methodist Protestant (A.U.M.P.) Church were held at Allen Chapel A.M.E. Floral tributes were many from the organizations to which she belonged.
Jul 25, 1887	At the Paradise Grove camp meeting Revs. C.W. Wayman, A.B. Wilson, and W. M. A. Cole preached. The John Wesley, Ebenezer, and Waverly praying bands conducted the prayer meetings.
Jul 25, 1887	The funeral of Edward Bryant, aged 40, who was accidently drowned from a scow while unloading coal at Taylor's oyster wharf, at the foot of Chester street, took place at Ebenezer A.M.E. Church.
Aug 16, 1887	A meeting of prominent citizens was held at Calvary Baptist Church, corner of Park avenue and Biddle street to discuss conditions in the State. A resolution was set forth that colored citizen were denied the right to teach their children in public schools; denied access to places of public entertainment such as public parks, the conservatory of music, ice cream salons; and, denied equal steamboat accommodations. They held that colored laborers were denied work on the public streets, lynched without any show of law, and discriminated against in the courts. They called for a Maryland Protective League to suppress these and similar evils.
Nov 16, 1887	The Monumental Literary and Scientific Association held a large meeting at Madison Street Presbyterian Church to hear C.H.J. Taylor, U.S. Minister to Liberia, a democrat appointed during President Cleveland's first term. He addressed the question of "Social Distinctions" with T .R. Ovelton, Revs. Weaver and Alexander, D.D. Dickson, I.O.B. Williams, and E.J. Waring.
Nov 23, 1887	John H. Biggus was lynched in Frederick County, Maryland. He proclaimed his innocence until he died.
Nov 29, 1887	The Brotherhood of Liberty of the United States met at Union Baptist Church, North street, Rev. J.C. Allen presiding. The object of the

	meeting was to secure colored people the rights guaranteed under the 14th and 15th amendments to the Constitution. The annual report stated in part that Maryland statutes are burdened with laws such as those which stand between colored lawyers and the Court of Appeals, and the bastardy laws, which do not recognize colored women as women. The board of public school commissioners of Baltimore city have an unwritten law which prohibits colored persons from teaching in colored schools. In consequence, those who have passed through universities and have obtained certificates as teachers are obliged to go to other States to pursue their calling.
Jan 26, 1888	The Maryland Colored Industrial Fair Association was incorporated for the purpose of holding a fair in Baltimore in the month of October every year to exhibit products made by skilled people in the State. The officers were Isaac Myers, president, Jacob A. Seaton, vice president, Thomas I. Hall, treasurer, Malachi Gibson, secretary, and Joseph Warren, treasurer. Several marshals were also appointed.
Feb 18, 1888	The Fourth District Republican League was organized with T.R. Ovelton as temporary president.
Mar 01, 1888	A committee composed of Dr. J. Marcus Cargill, Rev. James A. Scott, W.T. Wilkinson, John F. Driver, Charles H. Kerr, W. Ashbie Hawkins and others was appointed to present resolutions to the Dorchester County School Board asserting that it was unjust, unchristian and bad treatment to close colored schools three months earlier than white schools.
Jun 21, 1888	At the Republican National Convention in Chicago, Frederick Douglass received a vote in nomination for President of the United States.
Jun 22, 1888	Mayor Latrobe and other dignitaries attended the graduation of four women from the Baltimore Normal School for the education of colored teachers. Martha E. Owen delivered the salutatory and Lizzie Allen the valedictory. Sophia Bond and Kate A. Sheridan also received teachers' certificates.
Jul 23, 1888	The Senate authorized that one million dollars be appropriated to reimburse depositors of the Freedmen's Savings Bank and Trust Company for losses incurred by the bank's failure. The bill excluded payment to white depositors who were said to have wrecked the bank and confined payments to colored people who had been defrauded of their savings.
Aug 20, 1888	The camp meeting at Emory Grove was reached by many carriages and buggies in addition to arrivals by train. William Rudolph, with

	William B. Burke as organist, and four cornetists, W. H. Thomas, Monroe Ward, James Sanders, and little James Mitchell, conducted the music.
Aug 28, 1888	The clerk's office at Towsontown recorded a certificate of incorporation of the trustees of St. Stephens African Methodist Episcopal Church of Back River, Baltimore county.
Aug 28, 1888	Mt. Gilboa A.M.E. Church near Oella, Baltimore county, reopened following extensive renovations. Rev. John F. Wagoner was pastor. The trustees were Basil Burton, D. Holland, Nicholas Gibson, and William Ward. Next to Bethel Church, on Saratoga street in Baltimore, it was said to be the oldest church in the Baltimore Conference.
Sep 07, 1888	Hundreds gathered at Irving Park by invitation from the Brotherhood of Liberty to celebrate the abolition of "black laws" of Maryland. Men, women, and children from Baltimore, Washington, and surrounding counties enjoyed the all-day picnic and celebratory speeches.
Sep 10, 1888	The Society of St. Joseph founded St. Peter Claver Catholic Church on Fremont avenue, named after a Spanish missionary who devoted more than 40 years to missionary work among African slaves brought to Cartagena, Columbia in South America during the first half of the seventeenth century.
Oct 03, 1888	Colored people held their first industrial fair in Baltimore exhibiting more than two thousand articles representing the various industries in which they were engaged. These included exhibits of woodwork, farm products, mechanical inventions, paintings, drawings, needlework, and foods.
Oct 05, 1888	More than 3,000 tickets were sold to the industrial fair with excursions coming in from York, Pennsylvania, Hagerstown, Cambridge, and Rockville. The fair was also visited by a detachment of the Capital City Guard of Washington under the command of Col. C.F. Revells. They were later entertained by the Baltimore Rifles military company at Douglass Hall.
Oct 06, 1888	This was Children's Day at the industrial fair and 50 children from the Colored Deaf, Dumb, and Blind Asylum attended. Edward Stauffer serves as principal.
Oct 14, 1888	Among the 20,000 people who attended the industrial fair were the highest officials of the city and State, the Judges of the courts, and the leading educators of the day from President Gilman of Johns Hopkins University to the teachers of public schools.

Oct 23, 1888	At the annual meeting of the American Missionary Association, Daniel Hand gave $1,000,000 to be held in trust as the Daniel Hand Educational Fund for colored people.
Nov 12, 1888	Rev. John M. Collett, pastor of Ebenezer A.M.E. Church, preached to a large audience about the progress of colored people in the 25 years since Emancipation, crediting it to having a religious foundation. He pointed out the political positions and jobs held; the opening of schools and businesses; the publishing of newspapers and journals; and the beginning of building wealth in black communities.
Dec 11, 1888	Rev. J. H. Nutter, a professor of historical theology at Centenary Biblical Institute, complained of ill treatment by the Eastern Shore Steamboat Company.
Dec 11, 1888	U.S. District Court indictments were filed against Dr. R. Hall, registrar of voters, in a conspiracy to prevent colored men from voting.
Dec 29, 1888	The Maryland State Progressive Teachers Association headed by Prof J. H. Nutter reported that nearly 6,000 children in Baltimore City could not find accommodations in public schools. In the counties, 30,000 were deprived of a public education.
Jan 03, 1889	A new school being built on Carrollton avenue was planned to open in the fall and expected to require about 12 teachers. It was stated that all teachers in it shall be colored.
Jan 12, 1889	The first national gathering of colored Catholics was held in Washington, DC with the goal to unite them in a combined effort to promote their religious, social, and material progress, and to give assistance to the clergy in their work. Among the most noted delegates were Rev. Augustine Tolton, the only colored Catholic priest, and Daniel A. Rudd, editor of the *American Catholic Tribune*. Father Tolton officiated at the high mass which opened the congress. Cardinal Gibbons preached the sermon to a large crowd of white and colored attendants. Delegates from Maryland included Rev. Slattery of the Society of St. Joseph.[11]
Jan 30, 1889	Hon. Ezekiel E. Smith, United States minister to Liberia, wrote a letter to the American Colonization Society describing the ways in which immigrants from the United States had to adjust to life in Liberia. They had to learn the climate and seasons; the crops, such as wheat, apples, and peaches that cannot be successfully grown there; and, the customs of the people.

---

[11] Priests and brothers in the Society of St. Joseph are often referred to as Josephites.

Apr 10, 1889	Among those to be graduated at the Law School of the University of Maryland were Harry S. Cummings and Charles W. Johnson. Both received their early education in Baltimore schools and earned bachelor's degrees at Lincoln University in Pennsylvania.
May 10, 1889	On this date George "Spider" Anderson made history by riding Buddhist to victory in the Preakness, the first black jockey to do so, as recorded in the *Sun* on May 2, 1943.
Jun 29, 1889	Frederick Douglass was appointed minister resident and consul general of the United States to Hayti [Haiti]. A brief biography shows that he was born in 1817 in Maryland and escaped slavery at age 21. Fleeing to the North, he learned to read and soon became known as a fluent speaker on antislavery topics throughout New England and Great Britain. During the war, he urged the enlistment of colored troops and helped recruit them. He became interested in politics, has held several offices, and written several books.
Aug 29, 1889	A reception was held for Rev. Dr. D. P. Seaton, presiding elder of the Hagerstown district of the A.M.E. Church, who recently returned from Europe where he served as a delegate to an international Sunday school convention
Aug 29, 1889	Morrison Boyer fell from the third story window of a hay-packing business at No. 653 Cider Alley where he worked. He was removed to his home where he was attended to by doctors from the Maryland University Hospital.
Oct 05, 1889	Members of the Seventh Regiment of the United States Colored Troops who fought in the Civil War held their first reunion on the twenty-sixth anniversary of the regiment's organization. One hundred survivors of the approximate 1,000 men of Maryland who went into the war came to the Metropolitan M.E. Church on Orchard street for the reunion. Attendees heard a sermon by Rev. Charles G. Key, pastor of the church, and remarks by Dr. Alexander T. Augusta. Mayor Latrobe spoke followed by addresses from several of the group's white officers. The orator of the day was Attorney Everett J. Waring. At six in the evening a banquet was held in the church parlors. The officers told war stories and there was more speech-making.
Dec 30, 1889	The Brotherhood of Liberty published a book entitled "Justice and Jurisprudence" which indicts the U.S. Supreme Court and other federal and state tribunals based on their supposed failure to give proper effect to the 13th, 14th and 15th amendments to the Constitution. The book was described as being "cleverly written, evincing much

	research, much scholarly attainment, and a vast deal of political purpose and bias."[12]
Mar 17, 1890	At the Washington Conference of the M.E. church, a committee consisting of Revs. P. G. Walker, A. H. Robinson, N. M. Carroll, E. W. T. Peck, and I. L. Thomas was formed to prepare a history of the Conference from the time of its organization twenty-seven years ago. Bishop Foster delivered a sermon at the Conference before a large, racially-mixed congregation.
Mar 24, 1890	Cardinal Gibbons confirmed fifty persons at St. Peter Claver Catholic church.
Jun 23, 1890	When Rev. J.W. Norris declined to marry Charles Thomas and Lizzie Waller, the bride-to-be fainted and the groom-to-be had a spasm. The pastor later explained that he had met a Mrs. Charles Thomas and assumed her to be the groom's wife. He realized his mistake and made a lengthy explanation which the couple accepted. All was forgiven and Rev. Norris married the couple before a congregation of 1,500 at Trinity A.M.E. Church at Biddle street and Linden avenue.
Jun 27, 1890	Baltimore Normal School for the education of colored teachers held its closing exercises at Raine's Hall. Six students received teaching certificates; medals were awarded for deportment and attendance, and premiums for proficiency in study and penmanship.
Aug 14, 1890	Private John Gordon of the 25th Infantry won the department gold medal as the leader of ten marksmen on the Army's Department of Dakota team.
Sep 09, 1890	Frederick Douglass spoke at Wayman's Gove on the subject of Hayti [Haiti]. He was accompanied by several local clergy and by a man named Julius Matane who was said to be an exporter of Haiti's coffee, and a millionaire. He said that Haiti had sustained a government for more than seventy years. Twice England and France had tried to invade its territory but failed. The United Sates government refused to acknowledge the independence of Haiti until compelled to do so by force of right. He further said that with a population of only 800,000 it exported over $70,000,000 worth of produce.
Sep 30, 1890	Rev. Dr. W.T.D Clemm offered a resolution at the meeting of the Ministerial Union stating, "We have read with profound regret of the action of the regents of the Maryland Law School excluding two young men from its halls on account of color, and hereby earnestly request them to reconsider their actions and permit these young men

---

[12] See *Sun* dated March 1, 2020 for more information on this group.

	to re-enter and pursue their studies to graduation." The majority of members present refused to consider the resolution. The Ministerial Union was composed of all protestant denominations.
Oct 11, 1890	The Centenary Biblical Institute was renamed Morgan College in honor of Rev. Lyttleton F. Morgan who donated the land for the school and served as Chairman of the Board of Trustees from 1876 to 1886.
Nov 05, 1890	Harry S. Cummings won election to the First Branch of the Baltimore City Council as a republican from the eleventh ward, becoming the first man of color man to hold an elected office in Maryland. Born to free parents in 1864 and attending local schools, he entered Lincoln University in Chester County, Pennsylvania in 1886, and, in 1889, became one of two Negroes to graduate from Maryland University school of law. After 1889 the University excluded Negro students.
Jan 17, 1891	Several works donated to Johns Hopkins University included "Studies of The Negro in Maryland" by Jeffrey R. Brackett and works by James Birney who changed his views from slave-holding, to colonization, to abolitionism.
Jan 23, 1891	Charles W. Johnson and George M. Lane of Baltimore became the first Negros to argue before the Court of Appeals. The case involved Elizabeth Smith who was injured by a horse-drawn Central Railway vehicle and awarded $250 by the Superior Court.
Jan 27, 1891	The city mourned the death of a politically active and gifted leader, Isaac Myers. A caulker by trade, he organized a Colored Caulkers Trade Union which led to founding the Chesapeake Marine Railway and Drydock Company around 1865. It operated until 1884. He later organized other groups and worked as an inspector of bulk goods for the port.
May 13, 1891	Asbury Green was lynched by a mob of men wearing masks, said to be from the lower part of Queen Ann's County and Kent Island. It was believed that they wanted Green to receive the death penalty rather than the 21 years of imprisonment imposed by the court.
May 26, 1891	A Druid Hill avenue cable car ran over Edward Ringgold three days after the line started. He was the first person fatally injured by a rapid transit car in Baltimore.
Jul 29, 1891	Adjutant General Howard of the 4th battalion National Guard and Captain S. M. Hamilton of the second cavalry U.S.A. visited Camp Annapolis where the colored troops of the Maryland National Guard were enjoying a ten days' encampment. They found the camp in good shape and the men well-organized. Captain Hamilton had also been

	detailed by the War Department to inspect Camp Douglass at Loreley City. Governor Jackson was set to visit Annapolis later in the week. Capt. Spence of the Monumental Guards would be officer of the day, and Lieutenant Tilghman of the Baltimore Rifles and Alleghany Guards, officers of the guard. Archie Washington served as Drum Major. Brigadier-General Brown was also expected to visit.
Aug 11, 1891	Frederick Douglass, the United States minister to Hayti [Haiti] tendered his resignation to James Blaine, Secretary of State. He later commented that it was unwise to send a minister to a foreign country who does not speak its language. French is the language of Hayti.
Aug 25, 1891	Speaking at a camp meeting at Irving Park, Douglass said, "I would rather be a slave and have my leg fettered than be the master and have the other end of the chain on my conscience."
Sep 03, 1891	Councilman Cummings appointed Harry T. Pratt, son of Lewis Pratt, president of the Progressive Republican Club of the eleventh ward, to receive a 3-year scholarship to the Maryland Institute of Art and Design.
Sep 19, 1891	The estate of John H.B. Latrobe was valued at a quarter of a million dollars at his death. The only bequest except to those in his family was $1,000 to the American Colonization Society of which he had been president since 1853.
Dec 13, 1891	On this date, Charles R. Uncles became the first colored man ordained as a priest in the United States according to the *Sun* dated June 21, 1902. He was a member of the Society of St. Joseph.
Jan 27, 1882	The *New York Times* estimated that the number of emigrants who had departed from South Carolina was 10,000, two-thirds of whom were represented as able-bodied men above the age of 21.
Feb 23, 1892	One hundred seventy eight Negro men, women and children from the Indiana Territory seeking passage to Liberia became stranded in New York when the bark engaged by the Colonization Society could not accommodate them. They found refuge in a mission on Eighth avenue operated by Rev. Stephen Merritt. Charitable persons sent clothes and food.
Feb 26, 1892	The British steamship *Ethelgonda* arrived at Sparrows Point from Rio Marma with 3.2 tons of ore. She was a new vessel built at Whitby, England commanded by Captain C.V. Gooding, a native of Barbados. He was the first man of his race to visit this port as the master of a steamship.
Apr 08, 1892	The Colored Preachers Association was informed that mobs of white men in the South were subjecting Negroes to sudden and cruel death

	by rope, pistol, and being burned alive. The mobs had no fear of being punished by the law, and the Associated Press as well as local newspapers were silent on the issue. The preachers met at Bethel A.M.E. Church and offered a special prayer to Almighty God for deliverance from these atrocities. They also appealed to both races to hold a day of fasting and prayer on the last Sunday in May.
Apr 15, 1892	The John F. Slater Education Fund for Freedmen formed in 1882 reported that the fund would pay the salaries of teachers in the normal and industrial departments of several historically black colleges in the South. Each school would receive between $3,000 and $5,000.
Dec 22, 1892	Eighteen armed deputies were sent to the coal mines of Brown & Sons in Elkhorn, Pennsylvania to protect 150 Negroes who were working in the mines while white miners were on strike.
Mar 15, 1893	Noted caterer Edward J. Faten served raw oysters, capons with mushrooms and French peas, broiled oysters, salad, ice cream, cakes, and coffee at the tenth annual meeting of the Baptist Social Union.
May 03, 1893	A meeting of the Monumental Literary and Scientific Association held at Grace Presbyterian Church denounced a movement of whites within the republican party to disenfranchise colored voters.
May 18, 1893	The law firm of Cummings and McGuinn represented Elijah Johnson when he sued the World Newspaper Company for libel.
Jun 16, 1893	Trustees of the Mt. Zion Colored Burial Ground on Bellona avenue near Govanstown were sued to recover damages alleged to have been caused by improper use of the grounds.
Jun 30, 1893	So well-prepared was the work of students at the Colored Manual Training School on South Fremont avenue that the best specimens were on exhibit at the World's Fair in Chicago.
Jul 09, 1893	On this date, Dr. Daniel Hale Williams performed surgery on Jim Cornish at Chicago's Provident Hospital which was the first well-documented surgery on the human heart. Dr. Williams had at one point attended the Stanton school, a Freedmen's Bureau school, in Annapolis.[13]
Jul 27, 1893	Rev. Dr. David A. Day (white) served as a Lutheran missionary in Liberia. His nearly self-supporting church of 150 members boasted a native pastor. Its farm exported 16,000 pounds of coffee to Baltimore annually.
Sep 05, 1893	The Bynum camp meeting in Harford County which had been going on for four weeks ended.

---

[13] See the *Sun*, December 1, 1985

Sep 05, 1893	Efforts began to rebuild Mt. Tabor Methodist Church in Anne Arundel county which had been destroyed by fire.
Dec 29, 1893	Zack Glasgow was drowned in the Wye River, off Bruff's Island. His partner in oystering, William Henry Jackson, had anchored his canoe off shore and Glasgow went off in a skiff to get him. Before reaching the canoe, Glasgow's skiff filled and he went down in seven-foot water and never came to the surface again,
May 02, 1894	Benjamin Tydings and Albert Dorsey were fined $1.00 for shooting craps on Sunday.
May 17, 1894	Eight medically-trained doctors and surgeons in Baltimore pooled their resources and purchased a three-story house at 419 Orchard street: Drs. W.T. Carr, Jr., J. D. Creditt, W.E. Harris, C.H. Fowler, J. Marcus Cargill, W.H. Thompson, R. M. Hall, and L.B. Dyer. On June 13th they opened Provident Hospital and free dispensary, the only place where they could freely practice their skills as physicians and healers.
May 19, 1894	In his will, philanthropist Johns Hopkins made provisions for an Asylum for Colored Orphans. It opened in 1874 with 26 children and moved on this date to a larger facility on Remington avenue.
Jun 18, 1894	Rev. Nathaniel Carter, a 28 year old theological student, was ordained to the Lutheran ministry at St. Peter's English Lutheran Church, Fayette and East streets. The services of ordination were conducted by Rev. W. N. Harley, superintendent of colored missions. Carter had been teaching at Our Saviour Lutheran Orphanage for colored boys, Ivy Mill lane near Govanstown, and will be installed as pastor of the Church of Our Saviour, the only colored Lutheran Church in or near Baltimore.
Sep 12, 1894	The Baltimore County Industrial Association held a fair at Timonium fairgrounds that featured exhibits and displays of breads, cakes, pies, vegetables, fruits, wine, and preserves. A baseball game, horse races, and bicycle races were also held. Colored men owned the contesting horses in the half-mile running race.
Sep 15, 1894	At the closing session of the Potomac District Conference of the African Methodist Episcopal Church, the actions of Ida B. Wells in making a crusade in England against the lynching of colored men was endorsed. Rev. Dr. D.P. Seaton and Rev. John T. Jenifer submitted a series of resolutions formally commending her course.
Oct 05, 1894	The body of John Dorsey, the pugilist known as the Baltimore Spider, was found floating in the North River in New York. He had fallen off

	an excursion barge. He was a short, copper-colored boy and was dubbed "Spider" on account of his bow legs.
Oct 12, 1894	The Congress of Colored Catholics and the Convention of St. Peter Claver's Catholic Union adopted a resolution offered by Thomas W. Swann of Philadelphia endorsing the crusade of Ida B. Wells against lynching.
Oct 26, 1894	For the first time in Baltimore, Ida B. Wells spoke at St. John African Methodist Episcopal Church. In her speech, she stated the following. "In 1891 there we 169 black men, women and children lynched; in 1892 there were 160, of whom 5 were women; in 1893 there we 159 who perished by lynching, four being women; in the first five months of the present year there were 50. These are some of the results of letting these lynchers do as they please." She was formerly a teacher and the editor of a newspaper in Memphis, Tennessee. She has lectured in New York, Chicago, Indianapolis, Des Moines, Iowa and Philadelphia.
Nov 05, 1894	Charles V. Plummer, appointed in 1884 as a Chaplain by President Chester Arthur, bore good character until he began to associate with enlisted men, one of the most grievous offenses of which an officer can be guilty. He was court-martialed, tried for intoxication, and dismissed from army service.[14]
Feb 20, 1895	Noted abolitionist, civil rights leader, writer, and public speaker, Frederick Douglass died of a heart attack at his home in Washington, D.C.
Feb 23, 1895	At a meeting led by Bishop Wayman at Bethel, arrangements were made for a delegation of fifty people from Baltimore to attend the funeral of Frederick Douglass in Washington, DC. They decided to later hold a memorial service. Comments eulogistic of the life of Mr. Douglass were made by Dr. H. J. Brown, W.F. Taylor, Rev. William Alexander and Malachi Gibson. Harry S. Cummings called attention to the fact that the North Carolina Legislature adjourned in honor of Mr. Douglass's death.
Mar 07, 1895	The St. James African Union Methodist Protestant (A.U.M.P.) Church in Towson held a memorial meeting in honor of the late Frederick Douglass. Benjamin Johnson presided. Several addresses were

[14] Rev. L. Jerome Fowler, a descendent of Chaplain Plummer, uncovered the court martial proceedings against Plummer and felt that the decision to issue a dishonorable discharge was unjust. An Army board agreed that racial bias played a part in the decision and reversed it, granting Plummer an honorable discharge. See the *Sun*, February 10, 2005.

	presented including one from H. Rufus White, principal of the Towson colored public school.
Apr 01, 1895	St. Emma's Industrial School for Colored Boys was opened in Powhatan County, Virginia for boys in Maryland and the South. The boys were to receive training in useful trades such as farming, carpentry, blacksmithing, bricklaying, the handling of steam engines and the management of grist, saw, and planing mills.
Jun 22, 1895	Mrs. Josephine Diebitsch-Peary wrote of an upcoming expedition to Greenland with her husband, Robert E. Peary. In speaking of members of the expedition, she said this of twenty-six-year-old Matthew A. Henson: He was with Mr. Peary in Nicaragua and was also in the Arctic expedition of 1891-1892. He is strong, active, intelligent and willing, and has demonstrated his ability to withstand cold and privation as well if not better than some of the white members of the expedition.
Jun 22, 1895	Two hours before the doors opened at Harris's Academy of Music, people had gathered outside. The seventh annual commencement of the Colored High School and the presentation of certificates of proficiency to students of the Colored Manual Training School were being held. Mayor Latrobe spoke at length stating that, "Thirty-four years ago there was a law in Maryland which prohibited colored citizens from receiving the benefits of public education." He also said that, as a representative of Baltimore in the Maryland legislature twenty-seven years earlier, he had opposed that law. He presented diplomas to thirteen students and certificates to three others. An address was delivered by Rev. Dr. T.H. Lee of Philadelphia who had attended school in Baltimore, and an honorary address by Heber Edward Wharton, a graduate.
Aug 24, 1895	From 300 to 1,000 letters could be placed on the receiving bed at a time, and others could be added using a new letter-stamping machine that was introduced at the New York post office.
Oct 09, 1895	Not long after Rev. Joseph Slattery decided to devote his life's work to Negro missions, he came across a poor colored woman whose compassion led her to shelter waifs and strays in her small house in an alley. She begged for provisions for them each day before she went to work. Rev. Slattery sought out help among friends, and on this date, Cardinal Gibbons formally opened St. Elizabeth's Home for Colored Infants in a new building on St. Paul street between Saratoga and Pleasant streets. Forty-one infants who had been temporarily sheltered in a house on Hoffman street provided by friends were to be brought

	to the Home which has accommodations for one-hundred fifty, to be operated by the Franciscan Sisters.
Oct 19, 1895	The Maryland Colored Sunday School convention was held at Sharp Street M.E. Church. The following officers were elected for the coming year. Rev. I. S. Lee, president; Revs. E. F. Eggleston, Harvey Johnson, Alfred Young, and others, vice presidents; I. R. Smith, Rosie Richardson, and J. C. Fortie, secretaries.
Nov 06, 1895	Dr. J. Marcus Cargill won election to the First Branch of the Baltimore City Council as a republican from the eleventh ward.
Nov 19, 1895	Following his speech on September 18th at the Cotton States and International Exposition where he asserted that blacks should join whites and work together in rebuilding the South rather than fight for political and citizenship rights, Booker T. Washington went on tour. On this date, he spoke at Brown Memorial Presbyterian Church. Following the Civil War, he had worked in coal mines and gone to school at night. Inspired by General Armstrong at Hampton, he desired to open a school at Tuskegee, Alabama and started with no property, one teacher, and thirty students. He said that "our institution now has sixty-nine teachers, 800 students, 1,800 acres of land, thirty-seven buildings, and property valued at $225,000. It has been our aim to make our own improvements and to make the institution self-supporting as far as possible….We teach farming, the principle supplies for the table being raised on the property; brickmaking, for our own use and to sell; brick-masonry, plastering, painting, shoe and harness-making, printing, and carpentry. The girls are taught housekeeping, sewing, millinery, laundering, dairying and horticulture. Nineteen States are represented by the students…We aim to have the students pay their personal expenses in cash and work at the institution. Outside of this, the expenses are $70,000 a year…Alabama appropriates $3,000 a year and we get $5,400 from the Slater Fund…." Prof. Washington went on to say that the school receives some contributions with the balance earned during his speaking engagements.
Feb 13, 1896	Isaac Murphy, considered by many to be the greatest American jockey of all times, died of heart disease. He won the Kentucky Derby in 1884, 1890, and 1891.
Mar 05, 1896	Baltimore County Commissioners appointed colored men to three jobs. Benjamin Hicks as sanitary officer; and Dennis Simms and S.E. Henson as lamplighters.

Mar 12, 1896	The Baltimore City Council agreed to a gradual replacement of white teachers in colored schools. But positions would first have to be found for displaced white teachers. Also, colored teachers would have to pass a special examination to qualify.
May 18, 1896	On this date the U.S. Supreme Court reached a decision in the case of *Plessy v. Ferguson* that upheld the constitutionality of racial segregation laws in public facilities as long as the segregated facilities were equal in quality. This became known as the doctrine of "separate but equal" and opened the floodgates for passage of such laws.
May 29, 1896	Sarah A. Baker, aged twenty-six years, died suddenly at her home, 207 Division street. She had lately been attended by Dr. G.W. Kennard, a "faith curist" and regular physician under the laws of the State. Dr. Kennard conducts Christ's Institute.
Jun 25, 1896	Baltimore Normal School for the education of colored teachers held its closing exercises at St. John A.M.E. Church. The valedictory was delivered by Cordelia E. Henry and the salutatory by Howard M. Gross. Attendance at the school increased from seven pupils in 1894 to the current 32.
Sep 28, 1896	Funeral services for Henry Hardy, aged sixty-eight, the long-time coachman of Mrs. Josiah Macy of New York, were conducted at Sharp Street Church. Mrs. Macy sent a check for $100 to defray the expenses of the funeral.
Dec 25, 1896	A dinner of turkey, cranberries, and other dainties was given by the managers to patients at Provident Hospital. They also received Christmas bags from the Hospital Relief Association of Maryland.
Mar 09, 1897	The Lexington Savings Bank, on North Eutaw street, went into receivership, following the unaccountable absence of its president and cashier, Everett J. Waring. The bank was incorporated in 1895, with a capital stock of $10,000, divided into 400 shares with a par value of $25 each. There were about 700 depositors.
Mar 24, 1897	George L. Stanley, former bookkeeper of the now defunct Lexington Savings Bank, called the central police station and withdrew the warrant he'd recently sworn out against the Everett J. Waring charging him with the embezzlement of $700. Waring heard of the warrant and surrendered. The next day he posted bail of $1,000 and was released. Through counsel, he stated he could make matters straight if he had a few days. The justice confirmed that Stanley appeared before him and withdrew his warrant thinking he could effect a satisfactory settlement.

Mar 27, 1897	Stockholders and depositors of the defunct Lexington Savings Bank met and determined to employ an attorney to look after their interests. Waring was presented by the grand jury on charges of embezzlement of $700 and a capias was issued for his arrest.
May 15, 1897	John W. Smith of Illinois and Richard C. Bundy of Ohio received appointments to the U.S. Naval Academy in Annapolis. A third applicant appointed by Congressman George H. White of North Carolina was expected.
Jun 03, 1897	St. Emma's Industrial School for Colored Boys held commencement exercises at its campus in Powhatan, Virginia. Students were mostly Catholic boys from Maryland, Virginia, and West Virginia.[15]
Jun 29, 1897	The Colored Citizens League drew fully 2,500 to a bull roast and barbecue at Kelly's Park on the Annapolis road. Tender pieces of meat were enjoyed by all, followed by addresses by William F. Sedgwick of Upper Marlboro and W.C. Chase, editor of the *Bee*, published in Washington. At night, a mass of dancers thronged a broad, elevated pavilion and gave rhythmic expression to the music of Prof. Frank Johnson's Empire Cornet Band.
Aug 13, 1897	The Free Excursion Society sponsored a trip to Chesterwood Park in Baltimore county for more than 1,500 children. The outing included fun, games, and refreshments. The Society gives three trips a year for colored children. A sermon was preached by Rev. W. M. Moorman of Centennial M.E. Church. Among the group were visitors from Washington, D.C. and New York.
Sep 01, 1897	Regarding appointments to the Naval Academy, "A well-posted colored man said: It is natural to suppose that the white students object to affiliating with a colored cadet, but he is... not only snubbed by the white students in ranks and at the dining table, where he is crowded out, but is neglected by the waiters, who seem to be jealous of his position and who make him as uncomfortable as possible."
Sep 06, 1897	The first colored Lutheran church, Our Savior, was dedicated. The exercises were well-attended by both colored and white, and will be held for ten days with a service each evening of which Lutheran clergy of the city will have charge. The church was built by the mission board of the General Synod of Ohio. It was proposed that, when the congregation raises money enough to pay for it, that the money be used in the building of another colored church. Rev. D. E Snapp, pastor of Martin Luther Church, was the prime mover in the

---

[15] See Baltimore *Sun* dated May 13, 1892.

	erection the new church and also a member of the board of control of colored missions, under whose auspices the church was erected.
Sep 13, 1897	Lutie A. Lytle became the first woman to receive a license to practice law in the State of Tennessee.
Sep 30, 1897	The St. Paul Commandery of the Knights of Templar of Philadelphia arrived by train in Baltimore and were met by representatives of the St. Joseph, Emmanuel, Rising Sun, and St. John Comrmanderies of Baltimore, and escorted to the Samaritan Temple, corner Calvert and Saratoga streets. Caterer Samuel E. Young prepared a feast that included roast beef, corned beef, ham turkey, chicken salad, fried chicken, oysters in many styles, potatoes, corn, tomatoes, celery, chow-chow, macaroni cross, noodle pyramid, horse cream, chicken cream, peaches, apples, grapes, bananas, a variety of cakes, pies, Roman punch, Blackberry romeo, and cigars. In the afternoon, the four commanderies, led by the Monumental Cornet Band, Prof. C.A. Johnson, leader, formed a line of march and paraded through several streets. The march, drill, and general appearance of the commanderies was exceptionally good and highly credible to all concerned,
Oct 23, 1897	At a meeting of the republican State central committee in support of republican candidates, John M. Langston stated that, when he was taking the oath of office as a member of Congress, every democratic member of the House of Representatives walked out saying that no colored man could represent a Virginia district in Congress. Langston served from September 1890 to March 1891.
Nov 22, 1897	Colonel J.F. Hanson, head of the white republican party in Georgia, made it understood that President McKinley was to make no more appointments of colored men to office in Georgia.
Nov 30, 1897	Councilman Dr. J. Marcus Cargill appointed Robert H. Clark, Jr. to the Maryland Institute of Art and Design. The Institute declined to receive him because of his color based on a bylaw the school had passed providing that only white pupils should be received. Councilman Cargill along with attorneys John Phelps and W. Ashbie Hawkins filed a petition with the Superior Court to compel the school to accept Clark. The Institutes' lawyers responded that when colored pupils had previously been received in the school, there followed a decrease in attendance, and that the presence of colored students threatened to destroy the school. Ten days later, Judge Ritchie dismissed the petition, and the school was not compelled to admit colored pupils.

Dec 02, 1897	Joseph Cooper was made superintendent of a new street-sweeping district with colored men to work under him.
Dec 10, 1897	Rev. S.T. Tice, Attorney Richard E. King, Louis Chase, James E. Howard, and John Johnson of Annapolis forwarded a resolution to Congressman Sydney E. Mudd requesting that a colored youth be appointed to the U.S. Naval Academy and that a high school be established for colored children.
Dec 11, 1897	Councilman J. Marcus Cargill appointed Robert H. Clark, Jr. to be admitted as a pupil to the Maryland Institute. The school declined to admit him based on his color. A court suit resulted finding that the school, as a private institution, was not bound by the 14th amendment to the United States Constitution and not compelled to admit him.
Dec 20, 1897	After serving as a missionary in Liberia for twenty-three years, Rev. Dr. David A. Day passed. The mission was left in charge of Rev. August Pohlman of Baltimore.
Jan 31, 1898	Rabbi Guttmacher of the Baltimore Hebrew congregation, Madison avenue temple, submitted an article about political parties in Berlin, Germany and Vienna, Austria forming with an anti-Semitic program.
Feb 03, 1898	Catherine Taylor, aged forty-six years, wife of William Taylor, 538 Bruce street, was found lying dead across a chair yesterday afternoon. She had been alone in the house since 8 A.M. When discovered by her sister, Jane Jackson, she had probably been dead for several hours. She had heart trouble.
Feb 05, 1898	So determined were white citizens of Hogansville, Georgia not to conduct transactions with a Negro postmaster, they mailed their letters on trains. To avoid him delivering their mail, they had businessmen pick it up and it would be distributed by the former white official.
Feb 16, 1898	A marriage license was issued to John W. Jackson, 417 Dover street and Wilhelmina Jefferson, both of Baltimore.
Feb 23, 1898	Citizens of Lake City, South, Carolina, objecting to the appointment of a Negro postmaster, shot and killed him and the baby in his arms. His wife and three daughters were wounded as his house was riddled with bullets and set afire. Postmaster Baker and his baby were cremated in the fire.
Mar 16, 1898	A delegation including Bishop James A. Handy of the A.M.E. Church, Rev. G. F. Bragg, Episcopal rector in Baltimore, John H. Murphy, founder and editor of the Afro-American newspapers, and Wiley H. Bates, Alderman in the Annapolis City Council met with Governor Lowndes to enlist his influence in appropriating $100,000 for an additional manual training school in Maryland for colored children.

Apr 25, 1898	The *USS Maine* exploded in Cuba's Havana harbor on February 15th killing 360 American crewmen. Congress subsequently declared war on Spain. Believing Negroes to be immune from yellow fever and other tropical diseases, a Fourth Regiments of so-called Immunes was formed to fight in Cuba. It included troops from Maryland, the District of Columbia, and Virginia.
May 20, 1898	Willie Simms rode Sly Fox, a Maryland-born horse, to victory in the Preakness when it was held at Gravesend Racetrack in Brooklyn, New York, the only black jockey to win all three races in the Triple Crown, as recorded in the *Sun* on May 2, 1943.
Jun 07, 1898	A democratic candidate for mayor of Cumberland, Maryland, supported by Negroes, won the election and appointed Robert Snively as janitor of the station house and Richard Edwards as a policeman.
Jun 08, 1898	Joseph H. Lockerman passed the semi-annual teachers examination earning placement on the list for eligible English teachers.
Jun 10, 1898	A mass meeting was held at John Wesley M.E. Church to protest the lynching of Garfield King in Wicomico county and the instructions by Marshall Hamilton for the police department to use clubs on colored men.
Jun 27, 1898	Judson W. Lyons, Register of the United States Treasury, delivered the address to six graduates at the second annual commencement of Colored Polytechnic Institute.
Aug 12, 1898	The U.S. and Spain signed a Protocol of Peace ending the Spanish American War. Following the war, the U.S. ceded the Spanish-held possessions of Guam, Puerto Rico, and the Philippines.
Aug 29, 1898	Marshall W. "Major" Taylor achieved international prominence in the sport of bicycle racing. He established a new world's record riding a mile in 1.41 2-5 from a standing start.[16]
Oct 11, 1898	Bethel A.M.E. Church hosted a reception for Bishop Henry McNeal Turner of Atlanta upon his return from a successful missionary trip through South Africa and the Transvaal Republic. Other churches participating were Ebenezer, Waters Chapel, Allen Station, St. John, Trinity, Oak Street Station, St. Paul, Providence Mission, and Grace.
Oct 11, 1898	Wright Smith, a 56 year old Baltimore man had been lynched on September 2nd near Annapolis. Alderman Wiley H. Bates offered a Resolution in the City Council to censure it but the Council refused.
Oct 20, 1898	William H. Chadbourn, a republican "political boss", denounced Governor Daniel L. Russell of North Carolina for encouraging

---

[16] See the *Sun* dated Aug 24, 1975.

	Negroes to vote. He created a movement among merchants and mill-owners to replace Negro labor with white labor and to boycott products from Governor Russell's dairy farm.
Oct 26, 1898	The American Missionary Association reported that the Daniel Hand Educational Fund for Colored People aided thousands of worthy students and planted many schools. Boys have been taught woodworking, ironworking, architecture, and agriculture. Varied industries for girls were reportedly also taught.
Dec 27, 1898	On the day after Christmas, there were forty-two cases entered on the northwestern police station docket for rowdyism. They included disturbing the peace by fighting on the street, cursing and swearing and making unseemly noises, and assaults, shooting, cutting and striking.
Dec 27, 1898	The newly founded Colored Young Women's Christian Association at 346 W. Biddle street was planning to include a cooking school in its program.
Jan 31, 1899	The American Missionary Association reported on Negroes receiving an education in professional fields including theology, law, and medicine. They pointed out that the department of medicine at Howard University, located in Freedmen's hospital, had graduated 253 doctors. There were 400 lawyers practicing in all courts, and about 1,000 seminary-trained men.
May 03, 1899	Hiram Watty won election to the First Branch of the Baltimore City Council, a republican from the new Fourteenth ward.
Jun 02, 1899	Morgan College commencement was held at Sharp Street Memorial Church at Dolphin and Etting streets. The college president, Rev. Dr. Francis J. Wagner, conferred a degree of master of arts on George W.F. McMechen and bachelor of arts degrees on Emory Fennell, Martin Jennings, and McHenry Naylor.
Jun 23, 1899	Forty men under the leadership of Harry T. Pratt founded the Maryland Social Science League to help find meaningful work for the thousands of colored children in the city, only a third of whom attend school. Pratt, Wallis Lansey, and others opened a co-operative laundry to employ women and girls.
Jun 24, 1899	P.B.S. Pinchback, ex-Senator from Louisiana, delivered the address to six graduates at the fourth annual commencement of Colored Polytechnic Institute. Several students received honors for high grades and achievements.
Jul 15, 1899	[When violent winds and storms sent ships crashing to shore, a call for help went out to Life Saving Stations on shore. The Life Saving

	Station at Oregon Inlet in North Carolina manned by a colored crew is mentioned.][17]
Jul 29, 1899	Four men had been hanged on the gallows. Hundreds of family members and friends crowded around to see the body of Cornelius Gardner who was laid out in a family member's home. Undertaker Felix B. Pye handled the body which was to be buried at Bonnie Brae Cemetery. Mr. Myers and Mr. James had already been buried at Laurel Cemetery, their arrangements having been taken care of by Undertaker Hercules Ross. The body of Joseph Bryan was taken to Asbury Cemetery where services were conducted by Elizabeth Johnson of Asbury M.E. Church, assisted by Frances Wright of Waters A.M.E. Church. The guilt or innocence of each man was unclear.
Oct 05, 1899	Rev. N.M. Carroll, presiding elder of the South Baltimore district of the Washington Conference of the Methodist Episcopal Church, opened the annual conference at Centennial M.E. Church at Caroline and Bank streets. The South Baltimore district embraces counties in Maryland and Virginia and churches in Baltimore city. It has 6,365 members.
Nov 11, 1899	Boxer Joe Gans, known at the time as the greatest lightweight who ever lived, gave a champagne farewell dinner at the place of Mrs. Young, on Cortland street. Many guests were the leading members of the Williams & Walker Theatrical Company which had feted him in Chicago a year earlier. Gans had won his match with McFadden and was leaving town for his next match with Steven Crosby of Kentucky.
Nov 17, 1899	The cornerstone of the new Provident Hospital was laid at 413-415 W. Biddle street with elaborate ceremonies. The exercises were under the auspices of the Grand Lodge of Masons presided over by Dr. J. Marcus Cargill. General Latrobe gave an address and emphasized that the hospital was started during his term as Mayor. Members of the board of directors at the ceremonies included Dr. W.E. Harris, dean, Dr. Charles H. Fowler, and others The resident physician was Dr. Richard Johnson and the head nurse, Annie Henry. Attached to the new hospital is a training school for nurses.
Mar 31, 1900	Henry P. Cheatham of North Carolina held a federal appointment as Recorder of Deeds of the District of Columbia.
Apr 12, 1900	While driving a mule cart on Leadenhall street at the crossing near Ostend street, William H. Meyers of Claret alley was killed. A

---

[17] The *Sun*, February 22, 1998

	Baltimore and Ohio Railroad passenger engine struck the wheel of the cart and threw Mr. Meyers high into the air. He died instantly when his body stuck the ground.
Apr 21, 1900	Councilman Hiram Watty addressed attendees at the Baltimore Annual Conference of the A.M.E. Church at St. John on Lexington street to encourage members to send their children to the Colored Manual Training School in Baltimore. Rev. J. T. Jenifer commended the councilman for bringing this matter to their attention. Bishop Handy stated his regret that the compulsory education bill was not passed and also encouraged attendees to support Wilberforce College in Ohio.
Apr 23, 1900	Five young men were raised to deacon's orders, and one to elder's orders at the Conference. Bishop Handy ordained the young men, assisted by Bishop W. B. Derrick of New York. Rev. John Wesley Diggs who had served the church for 33 said he had broken down in health and could no longer serve.
May 03, 1900	There were only 18 Negro delegates among the 240 at the Republican State Convention in Raleigh, North Carolina while four years ago there were 180. The goal was to have no Negro nominees for office and none as delegates. There are 13 counties in North Carolina with Negro majorities
May 26, 1900	The Maryland and District of Columbia missionary Baptist Convention, in session at Macedonia Baptist Church, Saratoga street and Vincent Alley, adopted resolutions advising that the Church take a decided stand against the liquor traffic. Rev. I. Toliver of Washington said the liquor traffic was more degrading than any other evil.
Jun 29, 1900	The annual commencement of the Colored Normal[18] School was held at St. John A.M.E. Church on West Lexington street. Diplomas were awarded to Delcy J. Whyte, Bessie E. Hensen, Alverta V. Green, and Charles Wallace.
Jul 20, 1900	The question of assembling a constitutional convention drew attention to the amount of land in Virginia owned by Negroes. Figures from the Auditor's office showed that the race owned one-twenty-sixth of all land in Virginia. Therefore, property ownership as a requisite to the right of suffrage might not be feasible.
Jul 23, 1900	A large, well-attended funeral for Samuel W. Budd was held at Sharp Street A.M.E. Church in Sandy Spring, Maryland. A long-time blacksmith, he had inherited the business from his father, Perry Budd.

---

[18] This school, located at Cortland and Saratoga streets, is referred to as the Baltimore Normal School and the Baltimore Normal School for the education of colored teachers.

Aug 11, 1900	In a long letter to the editor, Francis B. Livesey of Sykesville proposed that Negroes hand in their registration and abandon the right to vote.
Aug 17, 1900	Bishop Henry McNeal Turner of the A.M.E. Church married Mrs. Harriet A. Wayman, a native of Baltimore. Bishop Turner has taken a prominent part in the political affairs in Georgia and had been appointed by President Lincoln as chaplain of the Thirty-first United States Colored Troops in 1863.
Oct 03, 1900	The fourth day of the annual registration in the 24 wards of the city resulted in the enrollment of 13,463 white and 3,123 colored voters. It was generally believed that there will be more than 115,000 names on the registration books before the last sitting.
Oct 06, 1900	"Prince Albert Hairston" a magician who claimed to have inherited occult powers through the spirit of an Egyptian woman who died 3,000 years ago was convicted in the police Court of practicing medicine without a license. A fine of $200 or imprisonment for six months in jail was imposed
Nov 24, 1900	George L. Pendleton was the first of his race to be admitted to the bar to practice law in Hagerstown, Maryland.
Jan 15, 1901	Twelve people applied to attend a training school for colored teachers. They were to be given instruction in teaching arithmetic, English, history, geography, mathematics, and physics in classes held at the Colored High and Grammar School.
Jan 26, 1901	In a letter to the editor, Rev. W.M. Alexander spoke against a mental qualification being proposed for Marylanders to vote.
Feb 22, 1901	James T. Booker died in the City Jail. He had been committed of larceny a month earlier, and sentence was suspended pending a motion for a new trial.
Feb 27, 1901	In her will, Miss Isabella Morris left $500 to the Shelter for Aged and Infirm Colored Persons of Baltimore located on Biddle street. Miss Morris died on February 20 in her eighty-sixth year.
Apr 25, 1901	The body of Asbury Stepney was found in the Severn River. He had been last seen while oystering alone. His bateau was found containing his coat and oyster tongs near the narrows. It was unknown when the drowning occurred.
Apr 25, 1901	Hiram Watty, Republican candidate for re-election to the First Branch City Council from the new Seventeenth (old Fourteenth) ward, will be opposed by D.D. Dickson, a colored lawyer who filed to appear on the ballot as an independent candidate. This will split the colored vote giving Democrats a chance to win.

May 09, 1901	The Baltimore City School Board adopted a recommendation to consolidate the Colored High School and the Colored Polytechnic Institute.
Jun 01, 1901	Mrs. Harriet Allen, age 81, died at the Shelter for Aged and Infirm Colored people at No. 517 N. Biddle street.
Jun 20, 1901	The *Baltimore Colored Independent* newspaper impressed upon Negroes their obligation to lift themselves and better their condition by a more manly and self-respecting use of the ballot rather than depend upon a particular party. It pointed out that, when the republican party came into power in 1895-1896 and controlled every branch of State government, not a decent office was given to a black follower of the party and not a single law was enacted for the betterment of his condition.
Jul 25, 1901	A race backed by the American Bicycle Company and the National Cycling Association received entries for a race at the Harford Avenue Coliseum for 25 famous sprint cyclers. Among them was an entry for Major Taylor who, for the first time in Maryland, would be a colored man racing against white contestants.[19]
Sep 09, 1901	After the Army Reorganization Act of 1901, the question was raised as to whether the Secretary of War would embarrass the Army by detailing officers who had been chaplains in colored regiments to white regiments.
Oct 3, 1901	An assassin, Leon Czolgosz, shot two bullets wounding President William McKinley at the Pan-American Exposition in Buffalo, New York. James B. Parker claimed that he sprang upon Czolgosz and bore him to the ground, preventing him from firing a third shot. Parker came to be called "The man who saved McKinley" and spoke of the experience on this date at John Wesley M.E. Church to a racially mixed audience. Parker said he was the guest of Attorney Cummings. Rev. Dr. Ernest Lyon was Pastor. Unfortunately, the President died eight days after the shooting.
Oct 28, 1901	The *Sun* interviewed Mrs. Ida B. Wells-Barnett who had gained notoriety in Northern states and in England by her denunciations of lynching in the South. She had published a newspaper, *Free Speech*, in Memphis which reported her investigations into lynching and found that most Negroes who had been lynched were innocent. Her newspaper was wrecked and she was driven out of the city. She had

---

[19] See *The Sun*, Jun 27, 1992

	been lecturing since 1892 and was to speak at the Ebenezer A.M.E. Church at 18 West Montgomery street, near Charles.
Dec 07, 1901	A board of directors was being formed at the House of Reformation for Colored Boys in Cheltenham, and Mayor Thomas Hayes insisted that a colored man be on the board. However, the concern was that other members of the board would remonstrate against serving with a colored man. The Mayor asked City Councilman Hiram Watty to recommend someone for the position and he recommended former Councilman Harry S. Cummings.
Dec 12, 1901	St. Francis Convent held a double golden jubilee in honor of Sisters Theresa and Alphonse. Both had completed 50 years of service with the Catholic Oblate Sisters of Providence. Sister Theresa previously served as Mother Superior.
Dec 20, 1901	On the recommendation of Senator Jeter Prichard of North Carolina, President Roosevelt selected John C. Dancy to succeed Henry P. Cheatham as Recorder of Deeds of the District of Columbia.[20]
Feb 18, 1902	Thomas I. Hall died at his home at 1033 West Barre street. For the past eight years he had been the Most Excellent Grand High Priest of the National Order of Galilean Fishermen which boasted a membership of 35,000 in the West Indies and States of the Union. He was born in Baltimore and had been a member for 35 years. Services were held at John Wesley M.E. Church at Sharp and Montgomery streets.
Apr 18, 1902	The University of Harvard baseball team had a colored shortstop named Matthew. He was described as a good fellow, having brains and unusual ability as a ball player. However, knowing the prejudice that existed in Southern States against his race, it was decided not to play him in States below the Mason Dixon Line. Therefore, when the Harvard team played in Annapolis against the naval cadets, Matthew did not play.
Apr 21, 1902	The centennial celebration of the organization of Sharp Street Memorial M.E. Church which will last six weeks had begun. Committees were formed for invitations, entertainment, decorations,

---

[20] The Negro vote gave Senator Prichard his victory. However, as the movement strengthened to make the republican party "lily white," he switched loyalties.

	programs, solicitations, and souvenirs. Services were to be held each evening until May 30th for spiritual leaders, local dignitaries, and congregations throughout the city. The church choir was directed by William E. Simpson
Jun 21, 1902	Rev. J. Harry Dorsey was to be the second colored man ordained in the United States as a priest in the Catholic church at the hands of Cardinal Gibbons. He received his education at several places including St. Joseph's Seminary on Pennsylvania avenue under Rev. J.R. Slattery of the Society of St. Joseph who encouraged him to study for the priesthood. He will celebrate his first Mass at St. Francis Xavier Church at Calvert and Pleasant streets.
Jun 26, 1902	Prof. Hugh M. Browne, principal of the Colored High and Polytechnic School, resigned to take a position in Philadelphia as head of the Institute for Colored Youth, which operates under the auspices of the Society of Friends. Prof. Browne graduated from Howard University, took the three-years course in the Princeton Theological Seminary, then took the course in psychology at Edinburgh University and afterward spent two years in Germany. The School Board elected Dr. James H. N. Waring to succeed him. Dr. Waring received his education at Howard University and Oberlin College.
Aug 29, 1902	The Republican State Convention at Greensboro, N.C. was composed entirely of white men. Former Negro Congressmen H.P. Cheatham and J.E. O'Hara were in every instance defeated. All business was settled in caucus. Capt. Charles Price of Salisbury, chairman of the convention, congratulated the party on the elimination of the Negro from politics in North Carolina.
Oct 21, 1902	North Carolina Republicans trying to create a white Republican party in that State resented as an interference the activity taken by James S. Clarkson, former Chairman of the National Republican Committee. Early in the fall, the Convention had excluded colored men from participation. The Negroes did not take kindly to their exclusion and tried without success to place in nomination Post Master S. E. Dicks of Weldon in the Second Congressional district.
Jan 03, 1903	The fortieth anniversary of President Lincoln's Emancipation Proclamation was celebrated at Boston's Faneuil Hall.
Jan 10, 1903	Salisbury Colored Grammar School was designated to offer a course in industrial training at the beginning of the school year. The girls were to be taught cooking, washing, ironing, sewing, and general housework. The boys taught carpentry, iron work, mat and basket weaving, upholstery, chemistry of the soil, and farming. The chief

	difference between the industrial course for the colored children and the course in manual training for the white children was that the training for the white children emphasized the educational feature of the work, the handicraft taught stimulating the activity and development of the thinking power of the brain. The idea for the colored children was to give them groundwork for a trade. Wicomico leaders engaged two instructors, W.P. Todd and Miss E.B. Welbourne. W. P. Todd graduated from Hampton Normal School in Virginia, Lincoln University in Chester County, Pennsylvania, and the seminary course at the Rochester, New York University. Miss Welbourne was a graduate of Washington, DC schools and had considerable experience teaching in Washington City schools.
Jan 25, 1903	Dr. Madison C. Peters was to preach at the Macedonia Baptist Church, Saratoga and Vincent streets, at a union meeting of the nine colored Baptist churches in this city.
Feb 14, 1903	The Oblate Sisters of Providence were to receive about $13,000 under the will of Nancy Addison, age 90 and unmarried, who died at the Sisters' home on Chase Street where she had lived for about 10 years. She owned a house at 1409 Jefferson street and had been a housekeeper for 30 years at the residence of Cardinal Gibbons.
Apr 22, 1903	Solomon S. Oliver, an Ellicott City teacher, was summonsed to appear before the school board because he and other teachers had kept the colored schools open beyond the designated closing date of April 14th. Oliver responded that Attorney W. Ashbie Hawkins had initiated proceedings to require that the school year for colored children in Howard County be as long as the school year for white children. The teachers were allowed to continue until the proceedings came to a hearing.
Apr 23, 1903	Rev. Dr. Ernest Lyon, pastor of John Wesley M.E. Church, who was appointed Minister and Consul-General at Monrovia, Liberia by President Roosevelt, took the oath of office in the office of Attorney Harry S. Cummings, 225 N. Calvert street. It was witnessed by many including M.J. Naylor, City Councilman Hiram Watty, Cabell Calloway, Jr., and Rev. S. R. Hughes. Walter W. Lewis presented Minister Lyon with a small, jeweled national flag. He will leave for his new charge in June.
May 02, 1903	The Mutual Benefit Society for paying sick and death benefits was incorporated by Dr. Charles H. Fowler, Felix B. Pye, Edward Pye,

	Ananias Brown, Phillip H. Pratt, Harry O. Wilson, Julie E. Pye, and Minnie B. Williams.[21]
May 13, 1903	The Farmers' Institute held at Princess Anne Academy in Somerset county for the benefit of colored farmers was well attended. Men from adjoining counties and the Eastern Shore of Virginia also came. Prof. Frank Twigg, principal, delivered the welcome address, and Prof. H.J. Patterson of the Maryland Agricultural College and William L. Amos, director of Maryland institutes, gave valuable assistance.
Aug 03, 1903	Race prejudice in the U.S. Navy was so strong that many sought to eliminate Negroes from service on war vessels. White sailors objected to any form of service that compelled them to regard Negroes as their equal. Officers came to the conclusion that it would be in the interest of good order and discipline onboard ship and on shore to organize a white navy and allow blacks to disappear from service.
Nov 22, 1903	The Feast of St. Elizabeth, patron saint of the Home for Colored Orphans and Foundlings, was observed with special religious ceremonies. The chapel was decorated, and at the early Mass, several children made their first communion. Cardinal Gibbons gave the benediction and delivered a little discourse on Charity. The Franciscan Sisters of Mill Hill, England oversee the Home. It shelters more than 100 children.
Jan 12, 1904	Former Attorney General John Poe proposed a change to the Constitution of Maryland that would disenfranchise Negro voters. The Poe Amendment was hotly debated but finally defeated in the November 1905 election. A second bill, the Strauss Amendment was also defeated.
Feb 07, 1904	[The Great Baltimore Fire broke out on this date, Sunday, at the John E. Hurst & Company building which caused an explosion that sent flames to adjacent buildings and continued to sweep throughout downtown. It raged for 30 hours and took 1,536 buildings and 2,500 businesses. When it was realized that that the blaze might overtake the *Sun* Iron building, editors furiously began seeking a place for safe storage of the valuable files of the paper bound in volumes from

---

[21] The Mutual Benefit Society opened in the rear of the undertaking establishment of Felix B. Pye, 102 E. Mulberry street and later moved to 712 S. Sharp street in the rear quarters of Dr. Fowler's office. The Helping Hand Building and Loan Association, along with a bank founded by Mr. Wilson, financed several large building projects in Baltimore including the Masonic Temple at McCulloh and Mosher sts, The Elks Hall on Hoffman street, and Shiloh Baptist, Psalmist Baptist, and Fountain Baptist Churches according to the Afro-American newspaper dated Feb 27, 1926.

	May 27, 1837, and other valuable effects. A special train of the Baltimore and Ohio Railroad was procured to take the material to Washington. The paper was published from there beginning on Monday, until April 7, 1904. Many personal accounts and memories of the Great Fire are recorded in the *Sun* especially on February 7, 1979. See also the *Sun* dated November 17, 1906.]
Feb 25, 1904	A Jim Crow bill introduced by Senator Brewington, a Democrat from Wicomico County, required racial separation in sitting, eating, and sleeping compartments on all rail cars and steamships that stopped in the State, nurses and attendants excluded. The bill did not apply to caboose cars on freight trains.
Feb 29, 1904	Pastors were urged by Rev. John Hurst of Waters A.M.E. to submit remarks against the Jim Crow disenfranchisement legislation being considered by the State. The goal was to appeal to the sense of justice of white people. Remarks were submitted by the Revs. W.M. Alexander, Rueben Armstrong, J. T. Jenifer, E. F. Eggleston, A. L. Gaines, George F. Bragg, L. L. Thomas, S.S. Wormley, and Rev. Dr. Waller.
Mar 03, 1904	Republican William Pairo who represented Baltimore's 4th District in the House of Delegates denounced the Democratic party when it passed the Jim Crow bill to separate races in Baltimore street cars.
Mar 18, 1904	Governor Warfield stamped his approval on the Jim Crow bills thus making the delegates in eastern counties and Southern Maryland happy. The law took effect July 1, 1904 and applied to the whole State.
Jul 20, 1904	Bricklayers at work on a large building at the Washington Barracks put down their trowels and went on strike because a Negro bricklayer was placed on the job. Captain John Sewell of the Corps of Engineers was in charge of the work. The matter was to be referred to the Bricklayers' Union.
July 20, 1904	The Century Encyclopedia states that "Jim Crow" is the title of a "dramatic song and negro dance brought out by Thomas D. Rice, the 'first negro minstrel' in Washington in 1835." (See entry for Oct 3, 1909.)
Jul 30, 1904	George W. Williams, who claimed to be from Baltimore, was accused of assaulting a woman in Harper's Ferry, West Virginia. The sheriff, his deputy, and two companies of militia escorted him to prison in Charlestown to keep him from being lynched. The militia planned to quarter in the courthouse and yard until the trial was held.

Aug 16, 1904	Two innocent men were killed by a mob that formed after a white woman said she had been assaulted by a Negro. The first was Scott Burton an aged man who was lynched and riddled with bullets. The second was William Donigan, a cobbler whose shop was within two blocks of the State House. The mob set fire to his shop and when he ran into the street, he was met with a shower of stones and bricks. When he staggered under the fusillade, he was seized and his throat cut. Governor Deneen said the actions of the mob were intolerable and inexcusable, and that wreaking vengeance on a race of people for the crime of one of its members was repugnant to all notions of law and justice. A full brigade of troops under the command of General E.C. Young was called to quell the violence. It occurred in Springfield, Illinois, where Abraham Lincoln began his political career.
Sep 02, 1904	H.H. Bart and his sister refused to move to the Jim Crow car when the train they were riding crossed over into Maryland. Both people and their baggage were removed from the train in Elkton, and a message sent to the local sheriff. Sheriff Biddle arrived and escorted them to jail. They had been traveling on the Philadelphia, Baltimore and Washington railroad.
Oct 26, 1904	The Helping Hand Savings and Loan Association was incorporated by Dr. Charles H. Fowler, Ananias Brown, Felix B. Pye, Charles Tolson, Phillip H. Pratt, Minnie B. Lewis, and Harry O. Wilson.
Jan 04, 1905	A book review of author Paul Lawrence Dunbar's "LI'L GAL" received favorable mention. The following love poem was quoted: "Oh, de weathah it is balmy an' de breeze is sighin' low, li'l gal, An' de mockin' bird is singin' in de locus' by de do', li'l gal; Dere's a hummin' an' a bummin' in de lan' from eas' to wes', I's a-sighin' fu' you, honey, an' I nevah know no res', Fu' dey's lots o' trouble brewing' an' a-stewin' in my bres', li'l gal." The reviewer described Dunbar's poetry as full of sweetness. The book was published by Dodd, Mead & Co.
Jan 10, 1905	A certified copy of the will of Nicholas H. Merriott was admitted to probate in the Orphans Court. He owned houses at 337, 340, and 342 Bruce street.
Feb 14, 1905	While driving a four-horse hay wagon across Baltimore street at Carey, Stephen Watkins, a farmer living near Savage, Howard county was struck by a street car. One horse was killed, another injured, and Watkins' right leg was broken. The Court of Common Pleas awarded in favor of Watkins against the United Railways and Electric Company. He received $1,800 in damages.

Mar 14, 1905	Two graduates of the Medico, Chirurgical and Theological College of Christ's Institute on Ensor street petitioned the Court of Common Pleas to be licensed to practice medicine, but the State Faculty refused to recognize the school.
Aug 11, 1905	A dispatch from Lexington, Kentucky notes the passing of the era of the black jockey. After the slaves were freed, it was difficult to get white jockeys to work alongside them, and opportunities for blacks eventually became unavailable. The article recounts the outstanding records of Isaac Murphy, Willie Simms, Pike Barnes, and other black jockeys who excelled in their sport.
Oct 21, 1905	"Hiram Watty dies suddenly," read the headline. His first political appointment was as inspector at the Custom House in 1870 while he attended Morgan College at night. Later he became messenger to the Collector of the Port. He served as deputy to Sheriff William F. Airey, and was then appointed inspector under the Treasury Department. Elected to the First Branch of the Baltimore City Council in 1899, he served three terms, followed by many other distinguished accomplishments.
Oct 26, 1905	At the Baltimore Synod of the Presbyterian Church, Rev. Dr. Henry Lindsay, a member of the Freedmen's Aid Society, spoke of President Roosevelt's visit to Tuskegee Institute. He said that Booker T. Washington was not giving students a proper education. He said students were receiving a scientific education and not enough religious training.
Jan 14, 1906	Negroes put into high office by President McKinley were slated to be discontinued at the end of their term and replaced by white men. This came at the insistence of politicians in South Carolina, Georgia, Florida, Arkansas, and Louisiana. It included Judson W. Lyons, Register of the Treasury, who was not to be reappointed to the position he had held for two terms.
Feb 01, 1906	The will of Mary A. Bordley admitted to probate in the Orphans Court gave $50 to Madison Street Presbyterian Church.
Feb 10, 1906	A Jim Crow bill sponsored by William E. Barrett of Newport News passed in Virginia's House of Delegates. It applied to the entire State.
Jul 08, 1906	Delegate George R. Percy of Dorchester County charged the Baltimore, Chesapeake and Atlantic Railway under the Jim Crow law with letting four colored passengers ride in the same car with white passengers. When Percy arrived in Salisbury, he swore out writs before Judge Turpin who issued one against the conductor and one

	against the railroad company and gave them to Wicomico County Sheriff, Elmer Bradley.
Aug 21, 1906	The United States 25th Infantry Regiment of colored soldiers was stationed at Fort Brown near Brownsville, Texas. At midnight on August 13th, shots fired on a street in Brownsville allegedly killed one white man and wounded another. The soldiers were accused by the mayor and townspeople of the shooting. While white commanders at Fort Brown said the soldiers were in their barracks sleeping at the time of the shooting, President Theodore Roosevelt, urged by prominent Texans, ordered the soldiers--167 in number--to be removed from Fort Brown, replaced by white troops, and dishonorably discharged.
Sep 26, 1906	After 10 Negroes had been killed; 15 taken to hospitals—five of whom were expected to die--; after others had been pulled from street cars and beaten and stomped to death; after windows had been broken and property damaged and Negroes had fled the city, Governor Terrell ordered the infantry to quell white mobsters in Atlanta who had been told that a white woman had been assaulted.
Sep 26, 1906	The emancipation celebration in Cumberland had about 60 vehicles in line besides a large cavalcade and a number of floats. A blacksmith had his forge on a wagon and was industriously engaged. On another wagon, a plasterer was busy mixing his trowel, and the bricklayers' trades were also represented. All of the carriages were gaily decorated and children rode on large picnic wagons. A company of boys gave a military drill as they proceeded along the march. The Odd Fellows in uniform also marched. Pictures of Abraham Lincoln were conspicuous. The parade proceeded to the baseball park where a barbecue was held, and there was a baseball game between the Cumberland and Frostburg teams.
Oct 24, 1906	A delegation of Philadelphia Negroes led by former Congressman George H. White of North Carolina who now resided in Philadelphia protested against the play "The Clansman" at the Walnut Street Theater. Mayor Weaver consulted with his City Solicitor, then issued an order suppressing further production of the play because it would create disorder and endanger lives.
Nov 18, 1906	Soldiers of the 25th Infantry Regiment hired Attorney James T. Green of Washington to take their case to court to determine whether President Roosevelt had exceeded his authority when he included in his order of dismissal the provision that the men should be deprived of their civil rights. While some military and Constitutional lawyers agreed that the he had, it was conceded that, by the Constitution he

	was the commander-in-chief of the army, and no one had the authority to interfere with carrying out his order. It was also noted that the President reached his decision individually based on the political aspects of the case and that the Secretary of War was not in entire sympathy with the President's action.
Dec 09, 1906	For the first time in history, the post of Register of the Treasury was held by a full-blooded Negro, William T. Vernon. Judson W. Lyons, who had retired from the position in June, was a mulatto. President Roosevelt chose Vernon for the position based on abilities he had demonstrated in his home State of Kansas.
Dec 21, 1906	Henry Davis was lynched in Anne Arundel County.[22]
Jan 11, 1907	Rev. Harvey Johnson of Union Baptist Church boarded a B & O Railroad train at Camden Station headed for Harper's Ferry. When told to go to the car set apart for Negroes, he refused and was ejected from the train. His attorney, W. Ashbie Hawkins, filed a claim in City Court for $1,000 in damages.
Jan 30, 1907	Senator Joseph Foraker of Ohio challenged President Roosevelt during a dinner about his decision to dishonorably discharge the soldiers accused of the shooting in Brownsville, Texas without a trial or hearing. The Senator specifically mentioned Mingo Sanders who had served in the military for 26 years and soon would have been entitled to a retirement pension and a right to end his days in the National Home for Soldiers.
Jan 30, 1907	The clerk of the Court of Common Pleas issued marriage licenses to Alexander Goodwin, 23 and Ella Avery, 28; John Lane, 25 and Florence Fleming, 19; Owens Murray, 40 and Charlotte Cooper, 25; and to Alexander H. Truxon, 21 and Bertina Scott, 20.
Feb 10, 1907	By his will, Charles D. Holt bequeathed to his servant Fannie E. Clark $5,000 and a farm in Prince George's County with all the farming implements, stocks, and furniture, in reward for her many years of faithful service and attention.
Feb 15, 1907	The Senate Committee on Military Affairs held an inquiry about the Brownsville Affair and upheld Roosevelt's decision.
Apr 19, 1907	Four colored officers served in the Army: Capt. Charles Young, (a graduate of West Point), Lieut. John E. Green, Lieut. Benjamin O. Davis, and Major John R. Lynch. Also, Rev. Oscar J.W. Scott of Washington, DC was appointed Chaplain.

---

[22]Four other men were lynched during this decade according to the *Baltimore Sun* dated Sep 30, 2018.

Apr 24, 1907	A gift of $1,000,000 for the establishment of a fund for schools for Negroes in the Southern United States was announced. The donor was Miss Anna T. Jeanes, a Quaker woman of Pennsylvania. Booker T. Washington of the Tuskegee Institute, and Hollis Burke Frissell, president of the Hampton Normal and Industrial Institute, were named as trustees of the fund, but neither of their schools was to share in the funds.[23]
Jun 14, 1907	For more than 35 years, the Free Excursion Society had been sponsoring trips aboard the iceboat *F.C. Latrobe* to Chesterwood, a park on Bear Creek in Baltimore County. Each year, there were 6 trips for white and 3 for colored groups of 1,300 or more women and children. Once they arrived at Chesterwood, the day would be spent playing on the playground eating, singing, dancing, and attending old time revival services. During the trip for colored on July 29, 1910, four ministers were on board and twenty-six babies were christened.
Jun 22, 1907	The nineteenth annual commencement of the Colored High and Training School was held at the Academy of Music before a large audience. Musical selections were given by the Mandolin Club and the speaker of the evening was Prof. Lewis B. Moore, dean of Teachers' College, Howard University. Among the list of those receiving diplomas presented by Mayor Mahool was Carl J. Murphy
Jul 01, 1907	A graduate of the Colored High School, Samuel R. Morsell, earned a degree of Bachelor of Arts at Oberlin College in Ohio.
Jul 30, 1907	James Reed was charged with the murder of a police officer, and lynched in Somerset County. Photographs of the lynching were made into souvenir postal cards for townspeople to send to relatives and friends across the country. The rope with which he was hanged was cut into small pieces and sold as souvenirs. Angry citizens later dug his body from his grave, made a large bonfire, riddled the body with bullets, and tossed it into a fire.
Aug 06, 1907	In a Republican primary election for delegates to the State convention from the seventeenth ward, Harry S. Cummings defeated Louis Davenport.
Oct 03, 1907	Over the course of ten years, the school board replaced white faculty with colored faculty in colored schools. All white teachers first had to be placed in white schools. And colored teachers, to qualify, had to have graduated from the Colored High and Training School. The

---

[23] The *Afro-American* dated Mar 28, 1914 gave a breakdown of the laudable way that the money was being spent.

	process was completed on this date. There were 14 colored schools in the city.
Nov 26, 1907	-An Industrial Fair held under the auspices of the United Grand Lodge of Colored Masons opened in Central Hall at Centre and Lombard streets. Among the lodges represented were those of Mount Horeb, Lebanon, King David, Hannibal, Zion, St. James, Friendship, Enterprise, St. John, King Solomon, and Mount Olive. Mayor Mahool delivered an address and commended the many exhibitors. The Fair continued until December 2nd.
Dec 29, 1907	A list of colored publications little known to the great mass of Baltimoreans were *The Crusader*, *The Baptist Messenger*, *The Dawn* and *The New Era*. Up to a short time ago *The Lancet* and *The Times-Union* were in existence.
Jan 11, 1908	A delegation of the Colored Law and Order League made up of Rev. John Hurst, Rev. John T. Jenifer, Josiah Diggs and W. Ashbie Hawkins called upon the Liquor License Board to better the conditions in Northwest Baltimore in the vicinity of Druid Hill and Pennsylvania avenues in which large numbers of colored people live. They wanted to begin with lessening the number of saloons in the neighborhood. They reported that in a district seven blocks long and two blocks wide there were 43 saloons. City health maps showed that the district was plagued by cases of tuberculosis. It furnished a disproportionate rate of criminals and was located near the Colored High and Training School and five primary schools, two of which were for white children. Many of the 12 churches in the district are within 300 feet of one or more of the saloons. Members of the League had held conferences with Dr. Gilman, formerly president of Johns Hopkins University, Judge Niles, and other prominent citizens who promised their help in seeking the betterment of conditions stated.
Mar 07, 1908	President Woodrow Wilson, an alumnus of Princeton University, later became the school's president. He attended the annual banquet of the Princeton Alumni Association of Maryland which was catered by Burgess & Hammond, a prominent Negro catering company.
Apr 02, 1908	Dr. James H. N. Waring, principal of the Colored High and Training School headed a delegation who protested to Governor Crothers against the "Jim Crow" bill requiring that separate seats be provided for the races on all electric lines extending more than 20 miles from the city.

Apr 23, 1908	In response to the Colored Law and Order League, which was supported by the Society for the Suppression of Vice, the Liquor Board has been asked to accept a rule that there shall be no saloon within 300 yards of a church or school, nor in an alley. This would reduce the number of saloons by 16.
Jul 25, 1908	The African country of Congo was said to be originally extremely hostile to foreigners but had been won to friendship largely through the efforts Negro missionary Rev. Dr. William Sheppard. President Theodore Roosevelt planned an expedition to Congo, and the Southern Presbyterian Mission Board extended an invitation to him to visit the territory of Bakuba that had been covered by its mission work. The Mission Board offered to assist the President in any way needed to make his visit pleasant and satisfactory.
Aug 17, 1908	The Westport Skating Rink on Fishhouse road near Maryland avenue was raided by police. The proprietor, John E. Kirby, and 21 Negroes were arrested. Kirby was charged with operating the skating rink for profit without a permit from authorities and for maintaining a disorderly house. He was given a hearing before a judge and released on $500 bail. The others who were arrested as witnesses were released in nominal bail for their appearance in court. Mr. Kirby furnished bail for the witnesses. Officers who took part in the raid had been watching establishments in hopes of catching violators of the Sunday liquor laws.
Aug 20, 1908	The ninth annual session of the National Negro Business League drew a large attendance at Sharp Street Memorial M.E. Church. The session was called to order by Harry T. Pratt, chairman of the local branch and Booker T. Washington addressed the group.
Aug 30, 1908	The presidential election found Negroes divided between voting for William Howard Taft, the choice of Roosevelt, a republican, and William Jennings Bryan, the democratic candidate. Those selected to hold federal offices such as William T. Vernon, John C. Dancy, and William H. Lewis supported Taft. On the other hand, leaders of the National Negro American Political League and the d, organized to support Bryan who was favored among liberal and populist elements of the democratic party.
Nov 16, 1908	The East Baltimore Station of the Methodist Episcopal church commemorated the 135th anniversary of the founding of Strawberry Alley Chapel. Rev. Joseph M. M. Gray was pastor and Mr. William Winks superintendent of Sunday School.

Dec 21, 1908	Dr. James H. N. Waring, a highly esteemed educator and activist, hired two pupils to be school janitors during the summer. They did not do the work so he did not pay them. The issue drew so much discussion and controversy among school board members that he apparently was forced to resign from his position of principal of the Colored High and Training School.
Dec 27, 1908	Jack Johnson became the first Negro to win the heavyweight championship of the world in boxing when he beat Tommy Burns in Sydney, Australia.
Apr 11, 1909	Marriage licenses were issued to David Hawkins, age 21 and Andena Lewis, age 21; Arthur H. Hughes, age 21 and Gertrude Hanson, age 20; William Lowery, 22 and Vinnie Burton, 21; and, Robert A. Proctor, 26 and Gertrude L. Harris, 28.
Jun 08, 1909	Between 1873 and 1899, three Negroes, William H. Butler, Wiley H. Bates,[24] and Thomas A. Thompson had been elected--from the predominantly Negro Fourth ward--to the City Council in Annapolis. A new registration law was passed stating that only those could vote who had voted in any State prior to 1868, or the descendants of such persons, and those assessed on the city tax books for not less than $500 worth of property. It was intended that this would "eliminate at least 60% of the Negro vote" and make the city safely Democratic.
Jun 18, 1909	While picking mulberries, the 10-year-old son of Joseph Lockerman, principal of the Colored High School, was shot and killed by an aged colored man.
Aug 18, 1909	Republicans held a "lily white" convention in Talbot County and did not invite Negro republicans or include them on their slate.
Sep 16, 1909	Nat C. Strong, president of the National Association of Colored Baseball Players of America, the Philadelphia Giants, and the Brooklyn Royal Giants came to Union League Park in Baltimore to play two games. "Home-run" Johnson who has been billed so often to play on Baltimore teams will play for Brooklyn.
Sep 16, 1909	Arctic explorer, Robert E. Peary, reached the North Pole on April 22nd and received many honors for his conquest. Only later did the public learn that a Negro, Matthew A. Henson, born in Charles County, Maryland, and four Greenland Eskimos reached the North Pole with him.
Oct 03, 1909	[Minstrelsy was a form of entertainment, primarily Southern, that often presented the Negro as foolish and ignorant. Jim Crow was a

---

[24] Mr. Bates continued to register and vote because he owned the required amount of property. According to the *Sun* dated December 9, 1984, in 1931 he donated $500 toward the purchase of land for a school for black children.

	minstrel character originated in 1833 whose name came to be applied to racist laws. An article on this date delves into the history of black-face art.]
Oct 29, 1909	A republican congress under President Ulysses S. Grant took away from all residents of the District of Columbia the right of suffrage in order to cut off the Negro vote. It was the first instance in Anglo-Saxon history where white men voluntarily surrendered their franchise rights in order to take the ballot from the Negro.[25]
Mar 29, 1910	The 3 protested yet another plan to deprive them of the right to vote in State and municipal elections. Both the Poe Amendment and the Strauss Amendment had been defeated in 1905. This effort, the Digges plan, was approved by the majority of members of the Legislature.
Apr 13, 1910	Governor Crothers did not sign the bills in support of the Diggs disenfranchise plan, and the plan was subsequently defeated.
Aug 10, 1910	The Edward James Faten Industrial, Agricultural and Collegiate Institute was provided for in Mr. Faten's will. A successful caterer, Faten bequeathed 307 acres in Charles and Prince George's counties for the school. He also provided for a home to shelter aged, infirm, and dependent Negroes.
Aug 22, 1910	When insurgents were sweeping on to the capital of Nicaragua, President Jose Madriz, his family, and others escaped to Corinto where James Weldon Johnson served as U.S. Consul.
Sep 05, 1910	In a campaign book, Republicans pointed out that their party had elected Abraham Lincoln and stood for equal justice. It stated that the Republican party had determined that the Confederacy should be destroyed and the Union preserved, which led to the freeing of 4,000,000 slaves. They later framed and passed the 13th, 14th, and 15th amendments confirming the civil and political rights of Afro-American people. Nearly 15,000 were said to have been given Government preferment for employment: eleven as ministers and consuls to foreign countries; eleven as officers in the army; and, 500 as postmasters. Fifteen received appointments by the President at the time. Others were employed in the Library of Congress, Patent Office, and departments such as Treasury, Interior, Justice, Agriculture, and the Government Printing Office. Democrats were denounced as being unfriendly to the race.

[25] See Dickson, Judge Harris, "The Negro in Politics", *Hampton's Magazine*, August 1909.

Oct 01, 1910	Former President Roosevelt appointed James C. Napier, a Tennessee politician, to serve as Register of the Treasury following the ouster of William T. Vernon after Vernon failed to line up with the administration of Governor Stubbs of Kansas in a bitterly-contested election.
Oct 22, 1910	The death of Elizabeth R. Cashner (white), former owner of Sotterly plantation, was reported. Sotterly was built in 1730 on the banks of the Patuxent River in St. Mary's County.[26]
Jan 01, 1911	George T. Bowen, the well-known caterer of the Athenaeum Club where prominent citizens of Baltimore met, died in his home on Linden avenue.
Jan 14, 1911	The death of former Mayor Ferdinand C. Latrobe was publicly mourned. He was instrumental in supporting colored teachers for colored schools, and he introduced and had passed in the Council an ordnance by which the Manual Training School for Colored Boys was established. He served three terms as Mayor.
Mar 01, 1911	Earning $5,000 a year, William H. Lewis of Boston held the highest paying federal position of anyone in his race when President Taft appointed him as Assistant Attorney General of the Department of Justice.
Apr 07, 1911	The Baltimore City Council passed, and Mayor Mahool later signed into law, the West Ordinance which called for the separation of races in residences, that is, blacks and whites could not live in the same city block.
May 09, 1911	The Maryland Legislature appropriated $5,000 to the Maryland Home for Friendless Colored Children to be used in 1911 and 1912. The home aims to receive and train children between the ages of 2 and 10. Rev. George F. Bragg serves a president.
Jun 05, 1911	Harry O. Wilson served as manager of the Mutual Benefit Society at Fayette and Pearl streets which was formed to aid the sick and bury the dead.
Jun 17, 1911	Dedication services of the new Maryland Normal and Industrial School for Colored Teachers, the first of its kind to be supported entirely by the State, were held at Jericho Park, Prince George's county. D.S.S. Goodloe will be principal of the new school.
Jun 24, 1911	James C. Napier, Register of the Treasury, gave the principle address at the 23rd commencement of the Baltimore Colored High School. He

---

[26] Several generations of slaves who served at Sotterly were recounted in the *Sun* on January 22, 1996.

	and Mayor Preston, who awarded the diplomas, were the guests of honor.
Jul 09, 1911	The First Separate Company of the Maryland National Guard distinguished itself by being the first of all volunteer organizations to go to camp when the call came in the Spanish American War. They drill in Moses Hall at 608 N. Eutaw street and are known for their strict, soldierly formation under the leadership of Captain Spencer. The company was organized as the Monumental City Guards on November 13, 1881 among waiters at Eutaw House and Barnum's Hotel, and were mustered into the militia of Maryland on February 20, 1882.
Oct 03, 1911	A playlet entitled "Mystic Gifts for the Pastor" was enacted by pupils of St. Francis Asylum for Colored Girls and visiting students to honor Cardinal Gibbons on the occasion of his double jubilee.
Dec 29, 1911	A small fire was caused in the home of William McGee, 620 S. Charles street at 7 o'clock by an overturned oil stove. The damage was slight.
Dec 30, 1911	St. Joseph's and St. Monica's Catholic churches will be consolidated under the pastor of St. Joseph's Rev. D. M. McCormick. Cardinal Gibbons initiated the change due to a shortage of priests in the diocese following the death of Rev. A. B. Leeson, former pastor of St. Monica's.
Aug 28, 1912	The American Bar Association admitted three Negro lawyers: William H. Lewis and William R. Wilson of Boston, and William R. Norris of Minneapolis.
Sep 02, 1912	Musical composer Samuel Coleridge-Taylor, son of an African father and English mother, died in London. At age five he began playing the violin and in 1890 entered the Royal College of Music where he began to develop his numerous talents as a teacher, guest-conductor, and recitalist.[27]
Sep 14, 1912	The 50,000 Negroes registered to vote in Maryland were expected to vote republican in the presidential election in November, but democrat Woodrow Wilson won.
Nov 13, 1912	A notice was posted announcing the annual meeting of the Helping Hands Savings and Loan Association, N.E. corner Fayette and Pearl sts, Dec. 12, 1912, 4:30 P.M., H. O. Wilson, Sec.

---

[27] His father was a doctor but, when not allowed to practice in England, he returned to Africa. Coleridge-Taylor developed an appreciation for African American folk music and was well received when he toured the U.S. in 1904, 1906 and 1910. www.britannica.com/biography/Samuel-Coleridge-Taylor

Dec 08, 1912	Jane Hendricks brought a suit against the wife of William Joyce (white) to gain inheritance to a property on Argyle avenue. Hendricks and her ancestors had been slaves of the Joyces. Joyce, who followed his wife in death, died without a will making him entitled only to life interest in the property. The attorney for the Joyces contended that slaves were not allowed to marry and that they were mere chattels with no right of inheritance. The lawyers for Hendricks contended that her ancestors did marry and were not treated as chattel but lived a decent life. (See entry for March 21, 1914.)
Dec 11, 1912	In orderly procession, 160 children and 54 nuns of the Oblate Sisters of Providence marched from the convent on Chase street when a fire broke out on the fifth floor. Aged and invalid sisters were rescued by firemen. The nuns and girls were given refuge in the home of John Leonard, warden of the penitentiary. Cardinal Gibbons hurried to the scene and comforted them, stating that, "It was providential that no one was injured or no life was lost."
Jan 15, 1913	Boxer Jack Johnson was arrested for traveling with his wife from Pittsburgh to Chicago. He was later convicted under the Mann Act in what was widely considered a sham trial. The Mann Act had been passed in 1910 to outlaw transporting women across State lines for any immoral purpose, but it was also used for racist purposes, the motivation being, in Johnson's case, the public outrage over his marriages to white women.[28]
Mar 07, 1913	Several hundred residents of Northwest Baltimore appeared before the Liquor License Board to protest against the large number of saloons in that section of the city especially on Druid Hill and Pennsylvania avenues. A list of 54 saloons in that section was given to the board recently in a petition signed by many residents of the section or connected with the religious, charitable or educational institutions located in it. Dr. Howard A Kelly, one of the leaders of the movement, was among those who appeared to back the petition by their presence and words. Rev. George A. Griffin of the chapel of St. Mary on Orchard street spoke earnestly and strongly against the saloons and the bad influence they had on the people there. The board deferred action on the petition.
Mar 13, 1913	Harriet Tubman, an ex-slave, known as "The Moses of Her People" died at the Harriet Tubman Home for Indigent Aged Negroes in Auburn, New York at the approximate age of 93. Of pure Ashante blood, she was born on a plantation in Dorchester County Maryland.

[28] www.history.com/this-day-in-history/jack-johnson-wins-heavyweight-boxing-title

	When she was 13 years old, she showed her instinctive antagonism against her master by protesting the brutality of an overseer. The overseer knocked her down. She fell ill, and while confined to her cabin became very religious, developing an almost fanatic faith that carried her through dangers. She finally ran away and went North. It wasn't long before throughout the plantations of Maryland and Virginia were spread rewards for a Negro woman luring slaves away from their masters. The price for her capture rose to over $40,000 but she was never caught. She made over 19 trips to this area and led 300 Negroes to freedom. She started a fugitive slave settlement at Cape May, New Jersey in 1852. It was managed by her with the aid of Thomas Garett, the Quaker abolitionist of Wilmington, Delaware. She received help and support from many others including William H. Seward, Secretary of State under Lincoln.
Jul 28, 1913	Senator Vardaman of Mississippi led a movement in Congress to repeal the 14th and 15th amendments to the Constitution which included the right of Negro men to vote. He also vowed to fight every appointment of a Negro to a federal position.
Aug 11, 1913	Republican Governor William W. Holden of North Carolina was removed from office by a hostile Senate following his activities in putting down the Ku Klux Klan in 1870. Attempts were later made to impeach him, but he was allowed to resign.
Aug 21, 1913	What was regarded as a plain attempt to defeat the principle of race segregation came to light when it was made known that a house at 708 Madison avenue had been bought by Charles R. Shipley, a Negro caterer who will use it as his residence and place of business. The house was equipped with electric and gas fixtures, modern bathing facilities on the different floors, and white marble steps and trimmings. Residents of the neighborhood declared that, had they known the deal was pending, they would have clubbed together, bought the property, and saved the block from Negro invasion.
Sep 09, 1913	At the sixteenth national encampment of the Union, Capt. John C. Daley of the police in Washington attempted to introduce a resolution which was designed to segregate white and colored members of the Army and Navy Union. National Commander George R. Downs stated that the black man had won his right to be in the ranks of the army and navy and declared the resolution out of order.
Sep 26, 1913	Morgan College attempted to relocate to the Carroll property in Mount Washington but faced strong opposition from area residents. Rev. Dr. John O. Spencer, the school's president, announced that Andrew

	Carnegie had pledged to give $50,000 toward a building fund for the college with the provision that an equal amount would be raised by the school college. $25,000 has already been raised. Mr. Carnegie's gift depends in no way on the removal of the college to a new location. Several offers of other were have been made.
Mar 05, 1914	A 20-round prize fight at the Westport Skating Rink was interrupted when the attention of spectators was turned from the main bout to a free-for-all fight in the rink. Whites and Negroes mixing together in good fellowship swore and yelled as pandemonium broke out. Two white men and two Negro men were later taken to Mt. Winans Police Station and locked up on charges of disorderly conduct. The fight occurred during the tenth round of the bout between Young Sam Langford of New York and Frank Hunter of Baltimore, both Negroes. After the fight was awarded to Hunter, both whites and Negroes swarmed the ring and shook hands with the victor.
Mar 21, 1914	In a brief article, it was stated that John K. Shields, Chief Justice of the Supreme Court of Tennessee, decided that ex-slaves are not entitled to inherit and have "no inheritable blood." [The basis for his decision was not given however it appears to be in violation of the 14th amendment to the Constitution].
Oct 18, 1914	The dedication of the Seventh Day Adventist Church at Druid Hill avenue and Robert street took place on the 17th. Elder Roscoe T. Bear preached the dedicatory sermon and Elder Gustave R. Roberts served as pastor.
Jan 19, 1915	Attorney W.C. McCard was barred from representing cases before Justice McFaul after McCard insinuated that the judge was biased.
Feb 03, 1915	Dr. Albert T. Chambers, Dr. James M. Delevett and Dr. Arthur Barneveld prepared a list of 17 names of celebrities of African extraction for the 17 colored public schools of Baltimore. Some of the ones adopted for selection were: Paul Lawrence Dunbar, poet; Frederick Douglass, orator and United States Minister to the African Republic of Liberia; Benjamin Banneker (1731-1804), astronomer and philanthropist; Robert Brown Elliott, born in Boston in 1842, educated in Eton, England, and sent to Congress from South Carolina; Edward W. Dryden, author and teacher; Phyllis Wheatley, poetess; Frances Ellen Watkins Harper, poetess; Ira Aldridge (1804-1867), actor; Crispus Attucks, said to be the first American to die in the Revolution; George Lewis Ruffin, born in Richmond in 1834 climbing from the station of barber to the judiciary and serving in the

	Massachusetts Legislature; Samuel Coleridge-Taylor, born in London in 1875, composer of music; and Henry Ossawa Tanner, artist.
Mar 26, 1915	At a health conference held at Bethel A.M.E. Church, Druid Hill avenue and Lanvale street, Dr. Harry S. McCard pointed out that the high death rate among colored people had its roots in segregated living conditions and segregated hospitals that refused them treatment. The Commissioner of Health (white) Dr. Gorter spoke of the need for institutional care for tuberculosis suffers. Dr. W.E.B. DuBois was the principle speaker at the closing session stating that Negroes had left country life and been herded into small airless rooms and congested alleys with dangerous, unsanitary conditions. He called for work and recreation out of doors. Three thousand men and women attended the meeting.
Apr 07, 1915	Pullman sleeping car porters went on the witness stand before the United States Commission on Industrial Relations and told of how much the tipping system meant to them. They testified that their salary of $27.50 per month could not pay expenses on the road without the tips they receive, to say nothing of paying rents and maintaining families.
Jun 1, 1915	The Albrecht Athletic Club lost two games to the Black Sox, 5 to 2 and 5 to 3. (Team members are listed.)
Feb 27, 1916	The very popular film "Birth of a Nation" introduced new techniques in filmmaking, but presented Negroes as foolish and ignorant, and showed the Ku Klux Klan heroically rushing to the rescue of white women and children.
Apr 01, 1916	Attorney Warner T. McGuinn represented Burgess & Hammond, a prominent catering company, when, having prepared repasts for Mr. & Mrs. G.T.M. Gibson, the checks used to pay them were returned unpaid and marked "insufficient funds."
May 21, 1916	Baltimore's Negro pastors raised $580 in their churches to purchase a special Bible which they presented to President Lincoln at the White House on September 8, 1864. 'This," said Lincoln as he received the Bible, "is the best gift God has given to man." Sojourner Truth was present and Rev. S.W. Chase spoke for the delegation. At Lincoln's death, his son Robert gave the Bible to Fisk University in Nashville, Tennessee. [29]

---

[29] For more information and a list of contributors, see the *Afro-American* newspaper dated November 21, 1959 and *Baltimore Sun* dated July 12, 1987.

May 26, 1916	Dr. Robert R. Moton, said to be a full-blooded Negro, was installed as principal of Tuskegee Institute following the death in 1915 of Dr. Booker T. Washington.
May 31, 1916	East Brooklyn and the Baltimore Black Sox split even with Brooklyn taking the first game and Baltimore taking the second. The names of players are listed
Jun 29, 1916	A letter to the editor from attorney W. Ashbie Hawkins questioned why Maryland Negroes should bear arms in a threatened conflict with Mexico when they would only be assigned to do menials tasks for white soldiers. He also raised other concerns about the plight of Negroes.
Aug 27, 1916	A child was discovered to have infantile paralysis at St. Katherine's School, 2001 Druid Hill avenue, where 40 children attended. The school building was placed under quarantine and every Sunday-school in the city closed by the Health Commissioner Blake. Also, Beatrice Jones, 13 years old, developed suddenly what physicians said was a rapid case and became critically ill. She was moved to the Harriet Lane Home of Johns Hopkins Hospital and it was said she would not recover. Two additional patients, Catherine Lewis, age 7, of 1032 Stockton street, and a 3-week-old baby in the Campbell family at 1409 Mosher street were also stricken. Cases among white children were also reported. A list of 13 extra doctors was designated to help prevent the spread of the disease. They were on duty at railroad stations and steamboat wharves to examine children under 16 years coming to Baltimore from States where paralysis was prevalent.
Oct 29, 1916	The All Stars and Black Sox played at the Y.M.A.A. Park, Lombard and Sixteenth street in Highlandtown.
Nov 19, 1916	When St. Peters Protestant Episcopal Church at Druid Hill avenue and Lanvale street sold its edifice and joined Grace Church, Bethel A.M.E. sought to purchase it. $14,000 of the $75,000 purchase price had been raised including contributions from the Mayor and other prominent citizens. The colored citizens committee consisted of the pastor, Rev. J. W. Sanders, Bishop J. A. Johnson, Bishop John Hurst, Rev. D. G. Hill, H .O. Wilson, H. T. Pratt, and Harry S. Cummings. The church membership was 800.
Dec 30, 1916	The 25th year of the brilliant career of Rev. Charles R. Uncles was celebrated. The first Negro in this country to be ordained a priest in the Catholic Church, he taught Latin and French at Epiphany Apostolic College, the preparatory school for St. Joseph's Seminary.

Apr 6, 1917	"President Proclaims War" read the headline as Congress voted to declare war against Germany, and entered World War I.
May 8, 1917	Beginning in 1913, the trustees of Johns Hopkins Hospital began making a series of administrative decisions that led to the closing of the Johns Hopkins Asylum for Colored Orphans. On this date the deed was accomplished.[30]
Jul 29, 1917	Negro men, women, and children estimated to number 10,000 marched down 5th avenue in New York in a silent protest of racial violence.[31]
Sep 11, 1917	Mayor Preston and members of both branches of the City Council assembled at 1815 Druid Hill avenue and went in a body to Metropolitan M.E. Church to attend the funeral of their colleague, Harry S. Cummings. As the body lay in state at the Church, a constant stream of people passed by the coffin. Services included many local and out-of-state clergy, as well as a list of distinguished, honorary pallbearers and active pallbearers. The City Council, and the Criminal and Orphans Courts adjourned for the rest of the week out of respect for Cummings' memory, and the flag at City Hall was flown at half-mast. On the motion of Daniel C. Joseph, the seat and desk occupied by Cummings on the City Council will be draped in black for 15 days.
Apr 23, 1918	Frank A. Furst chaired a campaign to raise $100,000 for St. Elizabeth's Home for homeless colored orphans in Govans. An anonymous donor wanted to give $100 and he did so with a Liberty Bond thereby helping his country as well as the Home.
Jul 22, 1918	The War Camp Community Service Club for colored soldiers was formally opened in the building at 406 Orchard street known as Old St. Mary's Hall. A dance was held and music performed by the Jazz Band of the Thirty-first Company of the One Hundred and Fifty-fourth Depot Brigade.
Nov 10, 1918	All-star baseball teams from the Interclub and Semi-Pro Leagues and the Black Sox, colored champions of Maryland, will resume their seven-game series at Shamrock Park, Highlandtown.
Nov 11, 1918	The Allies and Germany signed an armistice ending fighting in World War I.
Jan 26, 1919	In Germany, wherever Negroes appeared in areas with the American Army of Occupation, they attracted great attention among the

[30] The Alan Mason Chesney Medical Archives of the Johns Hopkins Medical Institutions.

[31] In East St. Louis, Missouri, white rioters had killed more than 100 people, and more than 6,000 were burned out of their homes. www.washingtonpost.com/news/retropolis/wp/2017/07/28/google-memorializes-the-silent-parade-when-10000-black-people-protested-lynchings.

	civilians. In cities such as Coblenz and Treves [Trier], they drew crowds of German children.
Feb 17, 1919	Gov. Harrington appointed Rev. J. H. Nutter, Cora H. Furniss, Celeste Hayman, and Mary E. Bell to begin making arrangements to welcome the return of Maryland's colored troops from World War I. The receptions will be held in Baltimore and Princess Anne.
Apr 02, 1919	Citizens elected two Negroes, Warner T. McGuinn to represent them in the First Branch, 14th Ward of the Baltimore City Council and William L. Fitzgerald in First Branch, 17th Ward.
Apr 08, 1919	The avowed object if the North Stricker Street Association was to remove John N. Reynolds, colored, from living in the neighborhood and to prevent any other colored person from owning or renting property in the immediate vicinity.
Apr 12, 1919	The death of Rev. Dr. William M. Alexander, founder and pastor of 2,000 members of Sharon Baptist Church and who served as secretary of the Lott Carey Foreign Baptist Missions, was mourned. He had graduated from the Wayland Seminary and was prominent in the Brotherhood of Liberty which worked tirelessly in the interests of colored lawyers and school teachers.
May 31, 1919	A homecoming celebration in honor of the colored men of Washington county who served in World War I was held in Hagerstown under the auspices of the Colored Women's Council of Defense and the Western Maryland Colored Association.
June 23, 1919	Maryland's colored soldiers, members of the Eight Hundred and Eighth Pioneer Infantry, who received their training at Camp Meade, were officially welcomed by a delegation of relatives, clergy, and leading colored citizens of Baltimore when they arrived at Newport News, Virginia. Twelve hundreds of the 2,700 officers and men who composed the regiment were Marylanders. Gov. Harrington had placed John Berry, chairman of the colored section of the War Camp Community Service, in charge of preparing a reception and feast for the men. They had survived a gas attack by the Huns in France, and performed well. The Chaplain of the unit was Lieut. George A. Rosedom, formerly pastor of First Baptist Church of Baltimore.
Jun 25, 1919	Twenty-nine members of the Colored Teachers' Training School, where Joseph H. Lockerman served as principal, were graduated. The Lyric Theater was handsomely decorated for the occasion. John Denues supervised the music.
Sep 23, 1919	Morgan College trustees agreed to purchase the 40-acre Morton estate at Hillen road and Arlington avenue. Work was begun on a dormitory

	and on Carnegie Hall, a three-story and basement structure, 52 by 75 feet. Both were being constructed with stone taken from quarries on the Ivy Land tract.
Dec 30, 1919	About 200 teachers from throughout the State attended the opening of the annual session of the Maryland State Colored Teachers Association held at Pennsylvania Avenue A.M.E. Zion Church. Prof. J. W. Huffington, State Superintendent of colored schools and others delivered addresses.
Dec 31, 1919	At the conference of State and county officials held at Western High School, the salary schedule provided for lower pay for colored teachers than for white ones.
Apr 10, 1920	More than 250 children from schools in Waverly and Lauraville planted trees on Harford road near Herring Run in celebration of Arbor Day. After planting the trees the children tamped around the roots. Under the guidance of their teachers, they sang songs and performed recitations in connection with the black oaks, pin-oak, and maple that they planted.
May 21, 1920	The twentieth annual commencement exercises of the Medico, Chirurgical and Theological College of Christ's Institute at 704 N. Ensor street took place at the school auditorium. Dr. G.W. Kennard made an address and distributed diplomas to seven nurses. The degree of doctor of medicine was presented to Frank Puryear, and that of bachelor of theology to Simon P. Archer, all colored.
Jul 03, 1920	Rev. Ananias Brown, until his recent passing served as pastor of Leadenall Baptist Church, edited and published *The Baptist Messenger*, and was president of the Maryland Co-operative State Convention from 1900 to 1914.
Jul 28, 1920	The National Association of Teachers in Colored Schools were welcomed to Baltimore for their seventh annual meetings by Governor Ritchie, Mayor Broening, and City Councilman Warner T. McGuinn. They alternated meetings at Bethel A.M.E., New Trinity Baptist, and Morgan College. Dr. Robert R. Moton, principal of Tuskegee Institute and president of the National Negro Business League; and John M. Gandy of Petersburg, Virginia delivered principle addresses. Several sectional sessions were held in various neighborhood churches and at Morgan College. The final session ended with an afternoon excursion down the bay.
Jul 30, 1920	Dr. John F. Goucher, president of the board of trustees of Morgan College, addressed a group at the dedication of the main auditorium of the school at Hillen road and Arlington avenue. The dedication was in

	connection with the 17th annual meeting of the National Association of Teachers in Colored Schools, and the entire day was spent on the grounds. In the afternoon, Dr. John O. Spencer, Dr. John Manuel Gandy, president of the teachers association; Mrs. Mary McLeod Bethune, and several others spoke. Dr. Spencer conferred the degree if Doctor of Pedagogy on Dr. Gandy and Thomas H. Kiah, principal of Princess Anne Academy, a former pupil of Morgan.
Aug 03, 1920	Twenty thousand Negroes gathered at Madison Square Garden to hear Marcus Garvey, founder and president of the Universal Negro Improvement Association (UNIA) urge them to return to Africa. The first business meeting was to be held in Liberty Hall at 138th street, the heart of New York's Negro district. Garvey published a newspaper that proclaimed his views and owned the Black Star Line of steamships.[32]
Aug 17, 1920	The Independent Republican League, indignant with the refusal of Republican leaders to recognize them with patronage, formed to select Attorney W. Ashbie Hawkins as a candidate for the U.S. Senate over the white candidate, O.E. Weller. Hawkins was nominated by Attorney J. Stewart Davis. Arthur M. Bragg, Rev. George F. Bragg, Dr. J. R. L. Diggs, John H. Murphy, W. Norman Bishop, Attorney Davis, Linwood G. Koger, Dr. E.M. Boyle, and others led in forming the League.
Sep 11, 1920	Progress was made toward world-wide Christian cooperation at a meeting of delegates from the National Church Federation and other church bodies. Delegates from 15 countries attended the meeting in Geneva, Switzerland. Bishop John Hurst was in the delegation from Baltimore.
Oct 01, 1920	Baltimore's first municipal day nursery for colored children was opened at 1513 Presstman street under the auspices of the Bureau of Child Welfare. Children of women who work during the day will be cared for there.
Nov 17, 1920	The Women's Civic League and a delegation of Negroes complained that the School Board salary increases discriminated against Negro teachers. Mayor Broening agreed that there should be equal pay for equal work. The matter was to be taken up by the Board of Estimates.
Dec 01, 1920	Joseph E. Janney, secretary and treasurer of the House of Reformation for Colored Boys at Cheltenham where he had served for 30 years, died at his home on Park avenue.

[32] The Baltimore *Sun* dated Aug 19, 1987 reports that Rep Charles Rangel sponsored a resolution to exonerate Garvey because he was not guilty of any crime. See also the UNIA History Blog.

Jan 29, 1921	84,740 Negroes called Baltimore home in 1910. In 1920 the population had risen to 108,390 including those brought into the city by the annexation of parts of Baltimore and Anne Arundel counties.
Jan 30, 1921	Speaking at the Colored Young Men's Christian Association on Druid Hill avenue before Negro physicians, Dr. C. Hampson Jones, Commissioner of Health, reported that the death rate among Negroes from diseases such as tuberculosis, pneumonia, and influenza was much greater than that among whites.
Feb 04, 1921	Charles Ridge of Emmitsburg in Frederick county was arrested for permitting his son Stanley Washington Ridge, age 12, to remain away from school. The boy and his sister were sent to Annandale school but the question was raised as to whether the boy was white. He had a dark complexion, black eyes, and straight black hair contrasted with the fair complexion, blue eyes, and light hair of his sister. Three physicians were called to examine the boy and concluded that he was not white. A Judge suggested that the boy be sent to Pennsylvania where "mixed" schools existed.
Apr 03, 1921	A National Negro Health Week started in 1914 under the auspices of Tuskegee Institute. Since its establishment, according to the statistics of the Public Health Service, the death rate among Negroes had decreased. The reduction in infant mortality was especially noticeable. Ministers in Baltimore preached about public health on this day with an emphasis on better sanitation. A health issue was to be emphasized each day of the week by physicians and educators, ending on Saturday with a general clean-up day.
Apr 29, 1921	The sale of the Maryland Industrial Training School for Girls on N. Carey street, to the Washington Annual Conference of the Methodist Episcopal Church for a home for the aged and orphan asylum for colored people, was agreed to by the Board of Public Works.
Jun 02, 1921	Twenty hours of race rioting in Tulsa, Oklahoma caused the city to be blood-drenched and blackened by incendiary fires. It was eventually put under martial law. The homes of 1,500 Negroes, valued at $4,000,000, were burned along with the people in them. Major Charles W. Daley of the police force estimated the deaths to be 175.
Jun 26, 1921	A Grand Jury investigation following 20 hours of race rioting led to indictments against seven civilians and five of the city police including Chief John Gustafson. It further found that there were underlying causes of the riot, notably the spreading of racial equality doctrine among Negroes.

July 16, 1921	Testimony that members of the police force participated in the recent riots in Tulsa was introduced by the State in the trial of John A. Gustafson, suspended Chief of Police, on trial for removal from office.
Aug 19, 1921	Josiah Diggs, of the Fourteenth ward, filed to attend the Republican convention.
Oct 04, 1921	The International All-Stars, who played a series with the Orioles, were to play the Black Sox at Westport.
Oct 28, 1921	The Laurel Park steward charged Frankie Coltiletti as being responsible for the fall of Meuse, with Lee Coney, a colored jockey up, in the running of the fifth race. As a result, Coney was in a Baltimore hospital with a possible fracture of the skull.
Nov 20, 1921	George Young, always interested in books about his race, served for almost 20 years as a Pullman porter, and collected books at every stop. Young's Book Exchange in New York now houses rare books about Negroes such as Phyllis Wheatley's poems published in London in 1772, "Narrative of the Life of Frederick Douglass" published in 1849, and "Fetichism and Fetich Worshippers" published in 1885 which was the work of Rev. P. Baudin, a missionary. Young had the largest public collection of literature by and about Negroes gathered together anywhere.
Dec 06, 1921	A site at Carey, Baker, and Calhoun streets was selected for the new Colored High School.
Dec 18, 1921	The Census Bureau made public a report showing that on January 1, 1920 there were 10,381,309 Negroes in the United States proper.
Jan 05, 1922	Debate on the Dyer Anti-lynching bill got underway in the House despite a determined filibuster on the part of Democratic opponents to the measure. Three hours were spent on roll calls demanded by Representative Garrett, Tennessee Democratic leader, in a futile attempt to head off the discussion. Half of that time later was given over to debate by Representative Dyer, Republican, Missouri author of the bill, and Representative Sumners, Democrat, Texas, one of the leaders in the fight against it.
Mar 20, 1922	Plans were made by the National Urban League under the auspices of the Baltimore Interracial Committee to study industrial problems of the Negro in Baltimore. The survey would include the number of Negroes employed in various industries, their opportunities for advancement, the attitude of labor unions toward them, and the amount of wages. The goal of the Urban League was to improve relations between the races and eradicate racial injustices.

Apr 09, 1922	Hundreds attended the funeral of John H. Murphy, 81-year-old publisher of the Afro American newspaper for 26 years. Bishop John Hurst conducted services at Bethel A.M.E. Church. Soldiers of the First Separate Company of the Maryland National Guard were pallbearers while delegations from the Colored Mystic Shriners and the Grand Army of the Republic attended in uniform. Representatives from the National Negro Press Association also attended.
Nov 19, 1922	Using the term, "Georgia Jim Crow School Board," Negroes were threatening to withdraw their support from the Republican candidate for Mayor in the next election if one of them was not named to the Board. They also wanted equal salaries for school teachers without regard to color or sex, and a university and agricultural college for colored supported by the State.
Nov 29, 1922	The imperial wizard of the KKK said that it was up to the Klan "to preserve the nation in keeping alive the spirit of the white race and in seeing that it remains supreme."
Dec 02, 1922	That President Harding was a personal exponent of the Dyer Anti-Lynching bill was made known today at the White House simultaneously with the word that Republican leaders have in effect, abandoned the measure. The President, it was said, had no intention of making any comment bearing on the Democratic filibuster even if the G.O.P. had determined to carry on the fight for the measure. The Dyer bill was dead and no effort would be made to resuscitate it.
Feb 13, 1923	"The Great Game of Politics: Seven Ways in Which The South Disenfranchises The Negroes" is the title of Article X, a lengthy analysis which all should read in full.
Apr 05, 1923	The Association for the Study of Negro Life and History held its spring conference in Baltimore. The purpose of the organization was to study Negro life in all phases and periods; and to collect and preserve Negro history and folklore. Special attention was to be given to preparing young men for serious scientific work in the study of Negro life and history. Three fellowships of $500 a year each have been provided for this purpose. Sessions were to be held at Morgan College, Bethel A.M.E. Church, and the Douglas Theater. The president of the association was Prof. John R. Hawkins, and S.W. Rutherford its secretary-treasurer.
Apr 23, 1923	The Department of Agriculture surveyed Southern farming districts and found that there was a general movement of farmers to Northern industrial centers. Reasons included boll-weevil conditions last year which made cotton growing unprofitable, unrest among troops

	returning from the war who had experienced living conditions more to their liking, and a breakdown of the contract labor system.
Apr 25, 1923	Improvements to the sewage treatment systems at Crownsville State Hospital for the Negro Insane, and the newly opened tuberculosis hospital for Negroes at Henryton in Carroll county, have been completed.
May 09, 1923	In the Fourth District, Warner T. McGuinn of the Fourteenth ward and William J. Fitzgerald of the Seventeenth ward were defeated by Democrats leaving no Negroes on the City Council. Though their two wards in the Fourth District had a large colored population, the white Republicans in the Fourth District voted on color lines rather than on political lines giving Democrats the win. This was the first municipal election since 1906 in which no Negro was elected to the Council.
May 14, 1923	The Brooklyn Royal Giants took a double header against the Black Sox at Maryland Baseball Park. The Black Sox had such disappointing games that half the crowd left before they were over.
Jun 19, 1923	In an effort to revive the movement to have a Negro supervisor over all Negro schools including the Colored High School, Carl Murphy, editor of the Afro American newspaper, wrote a letter to Mayor Jackson. Mr. Francis A. Russell, brought to Baltimore from Cincinnati, was currently supervisor over the colored elementary schools. Mayor Broening wanted him placed in charge of the High School also, but the School Board failed to approve the recommendation.
Sep 23, 1923	The Real Estate Board of Baltimore indicated that new legislation must be passed to prevent the influx of Negroes from the South from moving into neighborhoods already occupied by white families. The sections of the city already given over to Negroes were overcrowded and there was nothing left to new arrivals but to attempt to live in sections occupied by whites. Numbers of complaints had been filed at the offices of the Real Estate Board.
Jan 17, 1924	Mayor Jackson selected members of an interracial committee who will make a plan, as suggested by the Real Estate Board, to keep Negroes from invading white districts or zones. The following were named to represent Negroes: Harry O. Wilson, Warner T. McGuinn, W. Ashbie Hawkins, William C. McCard, C.C. Fitzgerald, Dr. B.M. Rhetta, Truly Hatchett, Willard Allen, Rev. Ernest L. Williams, and J.N. Fortune.
Jan 26, 1924	Sam J. Bush, one of the cleverest steeplechase jockeys ever backed by Maryland, finished second twice in the Manly Memorial at Pimlico.

Aug 08, 1924	Baltimore was awarded second prize for clean-up work during National Negro Heath Week last April. The prizes are offered by the National Clean-up and Paint-up Bureau of St. Louis. They will be presented at the silver jubilee session of the National Business League in August in Chicago.
Sep 30, 1924	Florence Mills was featured in "Dixie to Broadway", a musical show that played at Baltimore's Academy of Music. Scenes were staged in Russia, China, and around the world.
Oct 03, 1924	Chief Judge James P. Gorter declared that the great majority of Negroes brought before him in the Criminal Court come from outside the city. It was exceptional, he said, when a colored person, a native of this city, came before him charged with a crime. Judge Gorter's observation was borne out by Peal Elliott a probation officer of the Supreme Bench who said, "I have noticed that poverty, poor living conditions and crime are to be found among the colored people who have moved up her from Southern sections."
Oct 06, 1924	The Colored World Series between the Negro National League champion, the Kansas City Monarchs, and the Eastern Colored League champion, the Hilldale Club, was played at the Maryland Baseball Park in Baltimore. Of the ten games played four different cities, the Monarchs won in Chicago. (The article lists the names of players.)
Nov 09, 1924	St. James African Protestant Episcopal Church at Park avenue and Preston street celebrated the one hundredth anniversary of its founding. The celebration will also include the thirty-third anniversary of the rectorship of Rev. Dr. George F. Bragg, Jr. in this parish, the only African church that was an integral part of the Protestant Episcopal diocese of Maryland. It was organized in 1824 by a colored clergyman, the Reverend William Levington of New York, as a missionary effort where a free school for African descendants was begun.
Jan 10, 1925	About 1,000 white persons and 2,000 Negroes attended the second annual musical festival of the Aeolian Choral Society which was held in the fifth Regiment Armory. The personnel of the chorus and band was composed entirely of Baltimoreans, and others trained under the direction of A. Jack Thomas, the general director of the Aeolian Conservatory of Music. He stands as one of the two members of his race to be graduated from the Institute of Musical Art in New York. More than 300 vocalists and 60 musicians took part. The concert was

	to benefit the Maryland Home for Friendless Colored Children in Catonsville.
Jun 07, 1925	Provisions placed in deeds conveying residential property which prohibit subsequent transfer of the property to Negroes are binding, the Court of appeals of the District of Columbia has held in affirming the decision of the Supreme Court of the District.
Jun 12, 1925	The Board of Estimates adopted a plan for equalizing the salaries of men and women teachers doing the same work in senior high schools. The appropriation for the current year was $50,000.
Jul 14, 1925	Firestone Rubber Company has joined the U.S. and Liberia in seeking a $500,000,000 loan to develop a rubber industry in Liberia under American control. The goal was to end British control of the industry in Liberia and for business interests to get an economic foothold in Africa.
Jul 25, 1925	Epiphany Apostolic College, the preparatory school for St. Joseph's Seminary, was relocated to a tract of 150 acres overlooking the Hudson in Newburgh, New York. St. Joseph's Seminary was moved to Washington, DC near Catholic University. Both schools were under the Society of St. Joseph.
Aug 01, 1925	Charles A. Oliver and Charles A. Spriggs were sworn into office as Aldermen in the Fourth wards of Annapolis. Both were elected on the Republican ticket.
Aug 18, 1925	First Sergeant Augustus Walley, retired, who enlisted at Reisterstown, Maryland, was awarded a silver star to be worn on his Spanish campaign ribbon, for gallantry in action against Spanish forces at Las Guasimas, Cuba in 1898.
Sep 08, 1925	Lawyers for colored teachers filed suit against the Mayor, City Council, Board of Estimates and the School Board asserting that no provision in the equalization of salaries for teachers in Baltimore City senior high schools had been made for them.
Nov 19, 1925	Following a recommendation by the grand jury, Maryland added a new building to Crownsville State Hospital for the Negro Insane. The new structure will provide facilities for an increase of 200 men and women.
Jan 30, 1926	Baltimore City Solicitor, Philip B. Periman, responded to the petition of colored teachers for inclusion in the appropriations for equalization of salaries. He answered that the ordinance was not passed upon the principle of equal pay for equal work. Rather, its purpose was to equalize salaries among white male and white female teachers.

	Colored schools were omitted because no discrimination existed between male and female teachers' salaries.
Feb 09, 1926	Claiming the racial integrity bill introduced in the Legislature would classify as "colored" some of the most distinguished families of Virginia, various patriotic societies prepared to fight the measure. The measure was being advocated by John Powell, Richmond pianist; Ernest Sevier Cox, ethnologist; and Dr. W.A. Plecker, State Registrar of Vital Statistics. It classes as "colored" all white persons with any known, demonstrable or ascertainable admixture of Indian or Negro blood and forbids their marriage to any white person.
Apr 10, 1926	The newly formed Maryland Interracial Commission held its first meeting at Douglass High School. The Commission was appointed by Governor Ritchie under provisions of a resolution of the General Assembly of 1924 to consider legislation concerning the welfare of colored people in Maryland.
Apr 23, 1926	Perhaps the most prestigious job in the old days was that of coachman: dignified and unbending gentlemen of color drawing the finest carriages through Druid Hill Park on a pleasant afternoon. They wore ornate coats, a cockaded silk hat, doeskin gloves, and bore a long-lashed whip. James Lomax proclaimed that their traditions are preserved nightly at the Doctors' Coachman's Association whose clubroom was at 1517 East Monument street.
May 30, 1926	The leadership of the Eastern Colored League will be decided when the Baltimore Black Sox and the Harrisburg Giants meet in a double bill at Maryland Park. These clubs have been staging a neck-and-neck race in the colored league so far this season. Both have won five and lost three games. Each team has a number of stars in its line-up.
Jun 19, 1926	During a special ceremony, the cornerstone of a new colored elementary school was held. Mayor Jackson, former Mayor Mahool, and chairman of Public Improvement Association delivered addresses. A band led by A. Jack Thomas and singing by the pupils of Schools No. 107 and 116 provided the music, and prayers were offered. The new school will be located on Preston street between Druid Hill and Pennsylvania avenues. Dr. Francis M. Wood served as supervisor of colored schools.

Sep 05, 1926	The branch of the Ku Klux Klan in Cumberland Maryland broke ties with the national organization denouncing it as being fraudulent and dishonest. The local organization comprised 2,200 members--men and women--who demanded a return of funds to the local treasury.
Sep 12, 1926	Newspaper men were the judges in a beauty contest at the Royal Theater on Pennsylvania avenue. Contestants in colorful outfits were Lillian Detty, Marie Hooper, Pearl Brooks, Palestine Williams, Pauline Clark, Helen Wye, and Helen Stevens who came out as trombones sobbed, drums throbbed, and the orchestra performed. A unanimous winner named Viola West with bobbed hair and personality, described as long, lean, and brown-skinned took the honors and prizes.
Jan 15, 1927	Repeal of the Jim Crow law, enacted in 1904 by the Legislature to require transportation companies to provide separate places for white and colored passengers, was recommended by the Maryland Interracial Commission in its report to Governor Ritchie and the General Assembly. They further asked that the school code be amended to provide the same minimum rate of pay in all public schools of the State. Dr. J.O. Spencer serves as chairman of the Commission.
Mar 08, 1927	The decision of the U.S. Supreme Court in holding unconstitutional the Texas statute which bars Negros from voting in Democratic primaries may have far-reaching effects. For example, the State constitution of Mississippi stipulates who shall be eligible to vote by numerous limitations such as payment of poll tax, ability to read and write, understanding of constitutional provisions, etc. It applies to Negroes buts does not name them.
May 01, 1927	Dr. John O. Spencer, president of Morgan College cited the contributions of diverse students who had attended the school. A young African woman, Cerelia Copper King, earned a degree, returned to Africa, and became the wife of Charles D. B. King, a president of Liberia. The dream of graduate Bishop W. Sampson Brooks, a missionary to Africa, to transform Monrovia College and Industrial Training School into a four year degree-granting institution, was realized in 1995. The first public high school for African Americans in Calvert County, which opened in 1938, was named after him. And William F. Crockett of Hawaii studied law at Morgan and became a judge in his home State.
Jun 16, 1927	Formal dedication exercises for the Samuel Coleridge-Taylor school at Preston street and Druid Hill avenue were held in the presence of

	1,500 pupils and friends. Speakers included former Mayors Broening and Mahool, Dr. Francis M. Wood, Supervisor of Colored Schools, and William Douglas Johnson, principal.
Jun 22, 1927	Forty-four students were graduated from the Fannie Jackson Coppin Normal School. Exercises were held at the Lyric Theater. Mayor Broening spoke at the exercises and told the audience of the need for a city auditorium that will seat 5,000 to 6,000 people. Only a limited number of tickets to the graduation could be issued because of limited seating. (Graduates are listed.)
Sep 30, 1927	The Madison Street Presbyterian Church at 104 West Madison street, erected nearly eighty-five years ago, has been sold. The trustees plan to purchase Evangelical Lutheran Church of the Incarnation on Madison avenue near North avenue for use of the congregation. Formerly known as the Madison Street Baptist Church, the edifice was purchased by trustees of the Madison Street Presbyterian Church in 1848 as a place of worship for the slaves of the congregations of the First and Central Presbyterian Churches.
Nov 03, 1927	A chorus of 600 voices intoned spirituals for which 200 musicians furnished music at the funeral of actress, singer and dancer, Florence Mills. Harry Burleigh, Abbie Mitchell, and Hal Johnson led the chorus, with Will Vodery conducting the musician. Mills' body lay in a $10,000 coffin as thousands of admirers both white and Negro streamed by the bier in tribute. They included housewives, merchants, school children, songwriters, members of the theatrical profession, and many others. She had recently returned from triumphs abroad and left a fortune of $250,000 to her family. Police reserves handled the crowd. Her funeral was said to be the largest in the history of Harlem.
Nov 24, 1927	Jamaica-born Marcus Garvey was charged with mail fraud while operating the Black Star Line of steamships and sent to the Federal penitentiary in Atlanta for five years. His sentence was commuted after he had served two years and he was deported to Jamaica as an "undesirable alien"
Nov 25, 1927	It was announced that a campaign to raise $150,000 for the remodeling, equipping, and furnishing of Provident Hospital will be launched at a dinner at the Hotel Emerson. The building to be updated is the old Union Protestant Infirmary. One of the principle speakers at the dinner is slated to be Dr. J. M. T. Finney, a member of the medical board at the hospital. Dr. Finney explained that there are now thirty-five patients in a space intended for only twenty, and no private rooms. With its Negro population of 121,295, Baltimore should have

	at least 1,213 bed to care for their needs. The Negro death rate is thirty-four percent higher than the national average.
Nov 29, 1927	Dr. Howard E. Young became the first Negro appointed as a member of the Jail Board. He was backed by Councilmen Warner T. McGuinn and Walter S. Emerson, and other Negro leaders in the community. They have also asked the Mayor to place a Negro on the School Board and the Board of Supervisors of City Charities.
Dec 13, 1927	A resolution requesting the board of managers of the House of Reformation at Cheltenham to employ Negro supervisors and teachers exclusively was adopted by the City Council at the request of Councilman Walter S. Emerson of the Fourth district.
Dec 20, 1927	With $423,703 in subscriptions and pledges to remodel, equip, and furnish Provident Hospital, the original goal to raise $150,000 was far exceeded. Of this amount, $140,007 was raised in by white organizations working in the campaign. $164,695.40 was reported at a meeting of the Negro workers at the Douglass High School. The hospital can realize the $110,000 in conditional gifts made by John D. Rockefeller, Jr., Julius Rosenwald, and an anonymous friend of the institution.
Dec 23, 1927	The football teams of Tuskegee Institute and Lincoln University usually played annually in Philadelphia. The expectation was that star athletes would move on to play professionally. However, some players now desire to become football coaches at high salaries. This has stirred up controversy between the two schools.

Index

92

95